Pocket
MARRAKESH

TOP SIGHTS • LOCAL LIFE • MADE EASY

In This Book

QuickStart Guide

Your keys to understanding the city – we help you decide what to do and how to do it

Need to Know
Tips for a smooth trip

Neighbourhoods
What's where

Explore Marrakesh

The best things to see and do, neighbourhood by neighbourhood

Top Sights
Make the most of your visit

Local Life
The insider's city

The Best of Marrakesh

The city's highlights in handy lists to help you plan

Best Walks
See the city on foot

Marrakesh's Best...
The best experiences

Survival Guide

Tips and tricks for a seamless, hassle-free city experience

Getting Around
Travel like a local

Essential Information
Including where to stay

Our selection of the city's best places to eat, drink and experience:

◉ **Sights**

✕ **Eating**

🍷 **Drinking**

✪ **Entertainment**

🔒 **Shopping**

These symbols give you the vital information for each listing:

📞 Telephone Numbers	👪 Family Friendly
⏱ Opening Hours	🐾 Pet-Friendly
P Parking	🚌 Bus
⊖ Nonsmoking	⛴ Ferry
@ Internet Access	M Metro
🛜 Wi-Fi Access	S Subway
🥗 Vegetarian Selection	⊖ London Tube
🍴 English-Language Menu	🚋 Tram
	🚆 Train

Find each listing quickly on maps for each neighbourhood:

Bar Hemingway

16 📍 Map p233, B2

Legend has it that Hemi self, wielding a machine ...rate this timber-pan...ered bar during ... showpiece is a ...en by Papa ar... town. Dress ...s.com; Hôtel Rit... ; ⏱6.30pm–2a...

6 ◉ Plac...

Lonely Planet's Marrakesh

Lonely Planet Pocket Guides are designed to get you straight to the heart of the city.

Inside you'll find all the must-see sights, plus tips to make your visit to each one really memorable. We've split the city into easy-to-navigate neighbourhoods and provided clear maps so you'll find your way around with ease. Our expert authors have searched out the best of the city: walks, food, nightlife and shopping, to name a few. Because you want to explore, our 'Local Life' pages will take you to some of the most exciting areas to experience the real Marrakesh.

And of course you'll find all the practical tips you need for a smooth trip: itineraries for short visits, how to get around, and how much to tip the guy who serves you a drink at the end of a long day's exploration.

It's your guarantee of a really great experience.

Our Promise

You can trust our travel information because Lonely Planet authors visit the places we write about, each and every edition. We never accept freebies for positive coverage, so you can rely on us to tell it like it is.

QuickStart Guide 7

Explore Marrakesh 21

Worth a Trip:

The Best of Marrakesh 121

Marrakesh's Best Walks

Marrakesh's Best ...

Survival Guide 143

QuickStart Guide

Welcome to Marrakesh

Prepare for your senses to be slapped. Musicians, snail-vendors and conjurers collide on Djemaa el-Fna, from where ochre-dusted lanes twist to curio-crammed souqs. While the city's thriving art scene and cafe culture generate a cosmopolitan buzz, it's the medina's heady scents and sounds that bedazzle, frazzle and enchant. Put on your pointy *babouches* (leather slippers) and dive in.

Stalls at the edge of Djemaa el-Fna (p24)
ALEX ANDREI/SHUTTERSTOCK ©

Marrakesh Top Sights

Djemaa el-Fna (p24)

If all the world's a stage, then Djemaa el-Fna is the grand finale, thrumming and shimmying to a mash-up of musicians and mayhem. The only option is to join in.

Ali ben Youssef Medersa (p60)

Putting your home-tiling efforts to shame since 1565, the Ali ben Youssef Medersa is Morocco's most beautiful building and a masterpiece of arabesque design.

Bahia Palace (p82)

This prime piece of 19th-century real estate was where Marrakesh's one percenters lived it up. Within its salons, Marrakshi artisans went to town in a frenzy of *zellij* (ceramic tile mosaic) and *zouak* (painted wood).

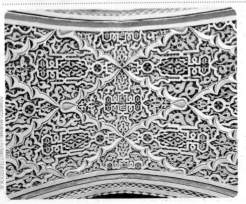

Saadian Tombs
(p84)

Making a statement in death, Sultan al-Mansour's mausoleum is a monumental blow-out of marble magnificence, and a fittingly exuberant exclamation mark to finish off the Saadian era's might.

Jardin Majorelle
(p102)

Take time out from monuments and medina dust in Jardin Majorelle, brought to life by painter Jacques Majorelle and later nurtured under the patronage of Yves Saint Laurent.

Maison de la Photographie (p64)

View Moroccan lifestyles and landscapes as captured through the early camera lens. The superb collection of vintage photography here unveils a vision of Morocco now consigned to history.

SARKUS/SHUTTERSTOCK ©

Dar Si Said (p86)

Moroccan craft abounds in this medina mansion. While the ground floor is home to the exhibits of the Museum of Moroccan Art collection, the *zouak* ceilings upstairs are the real show-stopper.

Musée de Marrakech (p62)

Take a peek at how Marrakshi high society once lived, swaddled in opulent luxury, inside this old palace that has thrown open its doors to the public.

MARTIN CHILD/ROBERT HARDING/GETTY IMAGES ©

JEFF HORNBAKER/WATER AGE FOTOSTOCK ©

Koutoubia Mosque (p26)

Guarding the entry to the medina since the Almohad era, the gold-hued stone minaret of the Koutoubia Mosque remains Marrakesh's most distinct and famous landmark.

Palmeraie (p118)

When the heat hits full-throttle, the shaded palm groves on the city's edge provide welcome relief, perfect for a camel ride or quad biking.

Marrakesh Local Life

Insider tips to help you find the real city

Marrakesh is more about ambience than a mere list of sights to tick off. Delve into the narrow lanes of the medina to explore how Marrakshis are merging modern life with ancient traditions.

Bab Doukkala Neighbourhood Stroll (p42)

▶ Quiet back lanes
▶ Residential life

Seek out the other face of the medina where touts, salespeople and tour groups disappear. Away from the main souqs you'll find the spindling *derbs* (alleys) where Marrakshis live without a trinket shop in sight.

Discovering the Heart of the Souqs (p66)

▶ Artisan workshops
▶ Local markets

Marrakesh's core of commerce offers more than Souq Semmarine and Souq el-Kebir. Meander through Souq Haddadine (Blacksmith's Souq) and explore the confines of the *qissariat* (covered markets) to discover the life behind the souvenir stalls.

Exploring Around Bab Debbagh (p78)

▶ Tanneries
▶ Marabout shrines

Stroll through the northeast slice of the medina where tanners continue their back-breaking trade and *marabouts* (saints) are venerated at local pilgrimage shrines. This corner of the old town exposes the time-honoured traditions still playing a role in modern Marrakshi life.

Guéliz Gallery Hop (p104)

▶ Art galleries
▶ Cafe culture

Head to Guéliz in the ville nouvelle (new town) for a completely different take on Marrakesh's cultural life. This is the hub of the city's growing contemporary-art scene, and has a clutch of art galleries and a thriving cafe culture to explore.

Moroccan *babouches* (leather slippers)

A local brassware stall

Other great places to experience the city like a local:

Mechoui Alley (p31)

Public hammams (p50)

The Mellah (p91)

Rue de la Kasbah (p91)

Snack al-Bahriya (p113)

Plats Haj Boujemaa (p110)

Rue el-Giza (p51)

I Limoni (p72)

Panna Gelato (p109)

Henna Cafe (p33)

Marrakesh Day Planner

Day One

☀ Spend the morning diving into the **central souqs** (p58) before they get swamped with crowds. Sniff out spice at **Place Rahba Kedima** (p70) and stop for a mid-morning mint-tea break at **Café des Épices** (p71). Afterwards experience a double whammy of architectural glory at the **Ali ben Youssef Medersa** (p60) and the **Musée de Marrakech** (p62) before moseying on to feast on couscous at **Naima** (p71) for lunch.

☀ Continue the historic finery theme in the medina's southern section, viewing the glorious ceilings of **Bahia Palace** (p82) and the dazzling **Saadian Tombs** (p84). Have a coffee break on the rooftop of the **Kasbah Cafe** (p95) before you wander back into the medina's central hub, stopping off to view the graceful interiors of the **Dar Si Said** (p86) along the way.

☾ Grab a spot on one of the cafe terraces of **Djemaa el-Fna** (p24) to capture photos of the floodlit **Koutoubia Minaret** (p26) and the full caboodle of the lit-up square as it fires into party mode. Duck away from the plaza for a tranquil riad courtyard dinner at **PepeNero** (p92), then launch yourself back into the Djemaa's madness to experience the best of the late-night carnival action.

Day Two

☀ Weave your way through the narrow alleys to see the blacksmiths hammering away in **Souq Haddadine** (p67) before viewing a slice of old Marrakesh in **Maison de la Photographie** (p64). Stop off at **Musée Boucharouite** (p69) for a peek at lesser-known Moroccan crafts before diving back into the souqs for a spot of shopping and lunch at **Kui-Zin** (p51).

☀ An afternoon in Mouassine beckons. Check out Marrakesh's caravan history in **Fondouq el-Amir** (p46) then admire the restored finery on show at the **Musée de Mouassine** (p45). Trawl for original gift ideas in the funky boutiques of **Souk Cherifa** (p55) and spot textile dyers at work in **Souq des Teinturiers** (p46). Take a break with a mint tea amid historic ambience at **Dar Cherifa** (p52), then scrub off the souq dust and rejuvenate aching joints with a hammam at **Le Bain Bleu** (p47).

☾ Head to Guéliz for top-notch tajine action at **Al Fassia** (p110) and afterwards stay in this part of town for a drink or two. For a casual, laid-back vibe head to **Café du Livre** (p115); for a fashion-forward, youthful crowd check out **Kechmara** (p105) or squeeze into tiny **68 Bar à Vin** (p114).

Short on time?
We've arranged Marrakesh's must-sees into these day-by-day itineraries to make sure you see the very best of the city in the time you have available.

Day Three

Grab a coffee and some macarons at **Pâtisserie Amandine** (p110) then head to **MACMA** (p108) to view its Orientalist art. Continue on arty ground with a stroll through the old painter abode of **Jardin Majorelle** (p102). Wrap yourself up in this tranquil haven of bamboo groves, birdsong and lashings of cobalt blue and brush up on Berber culture within the garden's fabulous **Musée Berbère** (p103). Afterwards dig into lunch at the **Amal Center** (p109) where Moroccan home cooking is at the menu's fore.

Head to the **kasbah** for an afternoon getting lost within the skinny alleyways of the *mellah* (Jewish quarter), and explore the city's Jewish history at the **Lazama Synagogue** (p90) and **Miaâra Jewish Cemetery** (p90). Then visit **Maison Tiskiwin** (p89) to view the ethnographic exhibits. Sit upon the ramparts surveying the ruins and their noisy storks in **Badi Palace** (p89) then hop across to **Kosybar** (p95) for a well-earned drink and more stork-watching on the rooftop.

As the sun sets, head to **Cafe Clock** (p91) for dinner if there is live music or a cultural event on, or dine on the rooftop at **Dar Anika** (p91).

Day Four

Discover some quieter medina action amid the *derbs* (alleys) that spiral off **Rue Bab Doukkala** before dropping into **Henna Cafe** (p43) for a mint tea and maybe a bit of henna art on your hands. Take another spin through the souqs to pick up souvenirs, then relax in the shady medina garden of **Le Jardin Secret** (p45).

Shopping and souqing over for the day, have lunch at **Souk Kafé** (p50) and then do as the Marrakshis do to beat the heat and head out of the centre for some serious poolside lounging. An afternoon of swimming and sunbathing in the palm-shaded haven of the **Beldi Country Club** (p139) is the perfect antidote for souq-weary feet.

After all that relaxation it's time to dive back into medina life by sampling some more of the magic of **Djemaa el-Fna**. Munch on snails (if you dare), watch music troupes and acrobats woo the punters, grab dinner one of the square's **food stalls** (p30) and soak up the full-on craziness of the open-air theatre for one last time.

Need to Know

**For more information,
see Survival Guide (p143)**

Currency
Moroccan dirham (Dh)

Language
Moroccan Arabic (Darija), Berber, French

Visas
Most nationalities do not require visas for
stays of up to 90 days.

Money
ATMS are widely available. Credit cards
are accepted in most midrange hotels and
above, and at top-end restaurants.

Mobile Phones
GSM phones work on roaming. For
unlocked phones, local mobile SIM cards
are a cheaper option.

Time
Western European Time (GMT/UTC + 0)

Tipping
Baksheesh (tipping) is an integral part of
Moroccan life. Tip 10% at restaurants; Dh3
to Dh5 for porters and baggage handlers; and
Dh2 to public toilet attendants.

① Before You Go

Your Daily Budget

Budget: Less than Dh750
▶ Double room: Dh250–Dh350
▶ Canteen tajine: Dh35–Dh50
▶ Djemaa el-Fna entertainment: free, plus tip

Midrange: Dh750–Dh1400
▶ Riad double room: Dh550–Dh750
▶ Three-course set lunch: Dh120–Dh170
▶ Half-day cycling tour: Dh350

Top end: over Dh1400
▶ Boutique-riad double room: from Dh800
▶ Dinner in palace-style restaurant: Dh300–Dh600
▶ Private hammam: from Dh250

Useful Websites

Marrakech Pocket (www.marrakechpocket.com) Marrakesh's monthly French-language listings guide.

Vivre Marrakech (www.vivre-marrakech.com) Events, new openings and listings.

Lonely Planet (www.lonelyplanet.com/morocco/marrakesh) Information, bookings and forum.

Advance Planning

Three months before Book riad accommodation; particularly important if travelling in high season.

One month before Organise activities such as cooking classes (most have limited space).

One day before Check the weather. Marrakesh gets colder than you think in winter, and fiercely hot in summer.

② Arriving in Marrakesh

Menara Airport is 6km southwest of town. Marrakesh's train station is conveniently located in Guéliz in the ville nouvelle. CTM buses arrive at the CTM bus station southwest of the train station while Supratours buses arrive at their small station around the corner from the train station entrance. If it's your first time in Marrakesh and you're staying in a medina riad, it's well worth booking the riad's taxi pick-up service to avoid getting lost on arrival.

✈ From Menara Airport

Airport bus 19 (Dh30) runs to Djemaa el-Fna and on to Guéliz every 30 minutes between 6.15am and 9.30pm. There are plentiful petits taxis waiting outside the arrivals hall; most charge inflated rates into the centre.

🚌 From the Train Station

Taxis tout for business by the exit. You need to bargain hard to get the price down to the metered rate of Dh20 to the medina. City buses 8 and 10 (Dh4) trundle between the station and Djemaa el-Fna every 20 minutes or so between 6am and 10pm.

🚌 From CTM and Supratours Bus Stations

Taxis wait inside the bus car parks. Most will quote Dh50 to Djemaa el-Fna. You can catch city bus 8 or 10 from nearby Ave Hassan II to the medina.

③ Getting Around

🏃 Walk

Most of the medina is a no-car zone so you need to get your walking shoes on to properly explore the lanes of Marrakesh's old city. If the weather is not too hot it's a straightforward 20- to 25-minute stroll from Djemaa el-Fna up Ave Mohammed V to the ville nouvelle.

🚗 Taxi

Metered rates for the city's beige petits taxis around town are between Dh8 and Dh20 with a Dh10 surcharge at night. Meters are supposed to be used but are often not. No trip within town should cost more than Dh20 by day and Dh30 at night.

Most drivers at taxi ranks near popular tourist locations such as Djemaa el-Fna and Jardin Majorelle quote exorbitant fees. Hail on the street for better rates.

If your party numbers more than three you must take a grand taxi (shared taxi), which always requires negotiation.

🚌 Bus

A variety of local buses zip between stops near Place de Foucauld (by Djemaa el-Fna) and the ville nouvelle at regular intervals throughout the day. All fares are Dh4.

Calèche

Horse-drawn carriage rides are a scenic option for trips between Djemaa el-Fna and sites such as Jardin Majorelle and the kasbah area. Standard prices for routes and hourly fees should be listed on each carriage.

Marrakesh Neighbourhoods

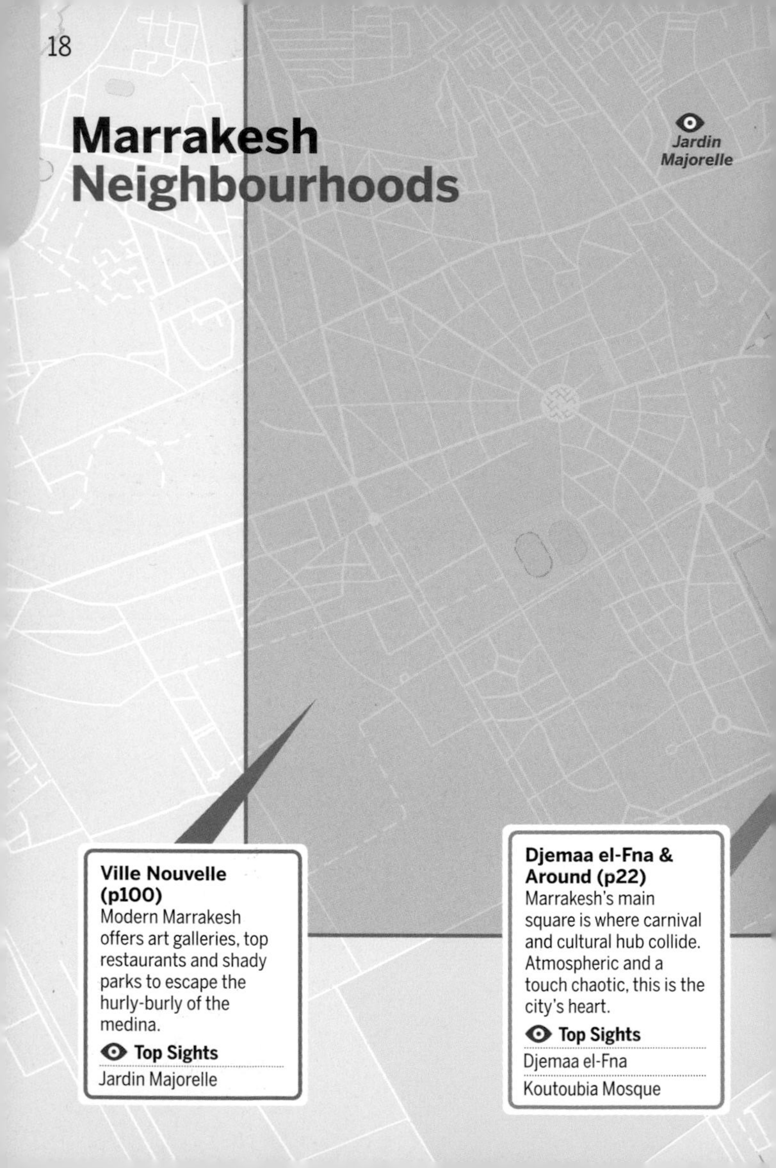

Jardin Majorelle

Ville Nouvelle (p100)

Modern Marrakesh offers art galleries, top restaurants and shady parks to escape the hurly-burly of the medina.

◉ Top Sights

Jardin Majorelle

Djemaa el-Fna & Around (p22)

Marrakesh's main square is where carnival and cultural hub collide. Atmospheric and a touch chaotic, this is the city's heart.

◉ Top Sights

Djemaa el-Fna

Koutoubia Mosque

Mouassine & Bab Doukkala (p40)
Funky boutiques and handicraft stores sit side by side in this medina neighbourhood of narrow passageways and blush-pink walls.

Worth a Trip
👁 **Top Sights**
Palmeraie

Central Souqs (p58)
Shop-till-you-drop souqs full of lively hustle and bustle and a magnificent *medersa*.

👁 **Top Sights**
Ali ben Youssef Medersa
Musée de Marrakech
Maison de la Photographie

Ali ben Youssef Medersa 👁
Musée de Marrakech
Maison de la Photographie 👁

Koutoubia Mosque 👁

Djemaa el-Fna 👁

Dar Si Said 👁

Bahia Palace 👁

Saadian Tombs 👁

Riads Zitoun & Kasbah (p80)
A walled city within a walled city. Marrakesh's grandest mansion architecture and a tomb almost worth dying for.

👁 **Top Sights**
Bahia Palace
Saadian Tombs
Dar Si Said

Explore
Marrakesh

Moroccan Berber carpets on display (p77)
JOHN COPLAND/SHUTTERSTOCK ©

Explore

Djemaa el-Fna & Around

Dorothy and Toto had their Oz; Alice had her wonderland; and now you can experience the out-of-this-world pandemonium that is Djemaa el-Fna. This chaotic hub is the heart and soul of Marrakesh, where snakes are charmed by day, music troupes shimmy and shake at night and visitors look on wide-eyed. Prepare to be swept up into the mayhem.

The Sights in a Day

☀ Say good morning to the mina-ret of the **Koutoubia Mosque** (p26) and check out the excavation site. Head to **Pâtisserie des Princes** (p32) for coffee and *pain au chocolat* then stroll across near-empty **Djemaa el-Fna** (p24) to see the square in its rare quiet moments.

☀ Sample lunch local-style with the Marrakshi speciality of *tanjia* (slow-cooked stew) at **Hadj Mustapha** (p31). Afterwards check out the eclectic exhibits of the **Heritage Museum** (p29) to discover Morocco's depth of history. Spend the rest of the afternoon mooching through nearby souqs to get a feel for what's on offer. Check out **Al Nour** (p37) for souvenirs supporting a worthy cause, and the cupboard-sized salons of **Fondouq el Ouarzazi** (p37) for Berber designs and Tuareg symbols.

☾ In the early evening head back to the Djemaa to watch the food stands set up for the night as the crowds start to stream in. As darkness falls, flit between Berber musicians, Gnaoua troupes and acrobats entertaining huddled circles. Eat dinner at one of the Djemaa's food stalls, and escape to a cafe rooftop if you start to suffer sensory overload.

👁 **Top Sights**

Djemaa el-Fna (p24)

Koutoubia Mosque (p26)

❤ **Best of Marrakesh**

Food

Le Tobsil (p30)

Hadj Mustapha (p31)

Gastro MK (p31)

Mechoui Alley (p31)

Shopping

Al Nour (p37)

Fondouq el Ouarzazi (p37)

Berber Culture

Djemaa el-Fna (p24)

Heritage Museum (p29)

Getting There

🚶 **Walk** From the kasbah area walk straight up via either Rue Riad Zitoun el-Jedid or Rue Riad Zitoun el-Kedim. Coming from Mouassine, the quickest route is south down Rue Mouassine.

🚕 **Taxi** From Guéliz, a taxi shouldn't cost more than Dh20.

🚌 **Bus** The most direct routes are via No 16 (from Guéliz) and No 11 (from Bab Doukkala).

Top Sights
Djemaa el-Fna

Roll up, roll up, for the greatest show on earth! Everywhere you look in Djemaa el-Fna, Marrakesh's main square, you'll discover drama in progress. By 10am the hoopla and *halqa* (street theatre) has already begun, but as the shadows fall the square revs up a notch and acrobats, musicians and entertainers keep the Djemaa pumping until late.

Map p28, D2

off Pl de Foucald

admission free

Musicians in Djemaa el-Fna

Morning Quiet

Stroll the Djemaa as it wakes up for the day to catch the plaza at its least frenetic. The orange-juice vendors are first on the scene as roving water sellers in fringed hats begin clanging brass cups together. Meanwhile, the earliest of the potion sellers and henna tattoo artists start setting up makeshift stalls under sunshades.

Lull before the Storm

The reedy whine of snake-charmer flutes is the Djemaa's soundtrack by mid-afternoon. While you're weaving your way across the square between a Gnaoua dance troupe and the fortune-teller stalls, an acrobat may cartwheel past and someone sporting fairy wings will probably stroll by. The Djemaa is finding its daily mojo.

Dinner at Djemaa

Pull up a pew at one of Djemaa el-Fna's food stalls to score ringside seats to the action. Chefs set up shop just before dusk and woo customers with grilled meats, tajines and more adventurous Marrakesh specialities such as snail soup, sheep's brains and skewered hearts. Now that's a meal to write home about.

The Carnival

At sunset the musicians start tuning up and locals flood into the square. Squeeze between clowns and cross-dressing belly dancers, pause at a boxing match and tap your toes to the music of the Berber troupes. The Djemaa doesn't knock off for the night until around 1am. When you need a break from the bedlam, head to a cafe rooftop and view the chaos from above.

☑ Top Tips

► Keep a stock of Dh1 coins on hand. You'll need them for tipping the performers. A few dirhams (a little more if you took photos) is all that's necessary when the hat comes around.

► Arrive early in the evening to nab prime seats on makeshift stools (women and elders get preference).

► Despite the alarmist warnings, your stomach should be fine if eating at the Djemaa night stalls. Clean your hands before eating, use your bread instead of rinsed utensils and stick to bottled water.

► Stay alert to motor-bikes and horse-drawn-carriage traffic, pickpockets and rogue gropers.

✕ Take a Break

If you feel your energy flagging, head to the terrace of Café de France (p33) for a mint tea.

For serious munching, follow your nose to Hadj Mustapha (p31), a basic canteen that dishes up one of the best *tanjias* in town.

Top Sights
Koutoubia Mosque

Five times a day the voice of the Koutoubia's muezzin rises above the Djemaa din, calling the faithful to prayer. The Koutoubia Mosque's minaret has been standing guard over the old city since the Almohads raised it in the 12th century. Today it's Marrakesh's most famous landmark. Gaze up in awe at the ornate decoration of the minaret's Almohad-era builders.

👁 Map p28, A4

cnr Rue el-Koutoubia & Ave Mohammed V

closed to non-Muslims

Crenellations to Inspire Copycats

They say imitation is the greatest compliment, and this 70m-high tower has quite the reputation as an architectural muse. It's the prototype for Seville's La Giralda and Rabat's Le Tour Hassan, as well as being a monumental cheat sheet of Moorish ornamentation. Crane your neck to check out the scalloped keystone arches and jagged *merlons* (crenellations).

Golden-Stoned Beauty

Originally the Koutoubia Mosque would have been covered in a layer of pink plaster, as Marrakesh's other medina mosques are decorated. After the restoration of the minaret in the 1990s, however, city authorities decided to maintain the minaret's natural golden-hued stone, a decision that allows the Koutoubia to stand out dramatically amid the old city's candy-tinted tones.

Legends of the Spire

The minaret is topped by a spire of copper balls, sticking up antenna-like and glinting in the sun. Once made from gold, local legend tells that the balls were 'gifted' to the mosque by the wife of Almohad sultan Yacoub al-Mansour, who melted down her jewellery as punishment after being spotted eating during Ramadan fasting hours.

Excavation Area

On the northwest side of the minaret are the ruins of the first mosque built on this spot, revealed by excavation work. This original mosque hadn't been properly aligned with Mecca, so the pious Almohads insisted on building a realigned one right next door. Walk behind the ruins for the best view of the excavation site.

☑ Top Tips

▶ Non-Muslims can't enter the mosque or minaret but will get great views of the minaret's stunning architecture from all angles by walking a full circuit around the complex, starting from the esplanade at the front.

▶ Come once during the day to photograph the minaret against a backdrop of blue sky, and then again just after sunset when the minaret's floodlights have been turned on.

▶ If you're feeling frazzled by all the Djemaa el-Fna action, the palm-tree-studded Koutoubia Gardens directly behind the mosque are a soothing respite.

✗ Take a Break

Refuel with a sugar fix at Pâtisserie des Princes (p32), lauded for its pastries.

For a refreshing mint tea with a view of the minaret, head across the road to Café el Koutoubia (p34).

RIADS
ZITOUN

Heritage
Museum 1

31

10

Derb Dabachi

Kennaria Dabachi

21

34

14

24

27

R. des Banques

Medina
Spa 3

35

22

25

7

17

26

Souq Ableuh

Souq Quessabine

32

**Djemaa
el-Fna**

9

23

R Riad Zitoun el-Kedim

R de la Recette

12

9

R Sidi Bouloukat

18

36

Souq Semmarine

Place Bab
Fteuh

30

5

R Bab Agnaou

13

11

R Mouassine

R Laksour

Brigade
Touristique

R Bani Marine

16

15

R Moulay Ismail

19

Derb Moulay
Abdellah
ben Hessaien

R el-Koutoubia

Place de
Foucauld

Airport
Bus 19

Ave el-Mouahidine

29

33

8

6

28

20

R Sidi el-Yamani

Bab Laksour

R Abbes Sebti

R Fatima Zohra

Ave Mohammed V

4
Koubba of
Fatima
Zohra

**Koutoubia
Mosque**

Koutoubia 2
Gardens

200 m
0.1 miles

CORBIS/SHUTTERSTOCK ©

Koutoubia Gardens, with a view to Koutoubia Mosque minaret

Sights

Heritage Museum
MUSEUM

1 ⊙ Map p28, E1

The Alouani Bibi family have thrown open the doors of this old riad to display their eclectic and fascinating collection of Moroccan artefacts. From Berber costumes and jewellery to Roman amphorae, the exhibits (all labelled in English and French) cover the wide arc of Moroccan history and culture. The rooftop cafe is a tranquil spot to relax in amid the souq hustle. (Musée du Patrimoine; www.heritagemuseummarrakech. com; 25 Zinkat Rahba; Dh30; ⊙9am-5pm)

Koutoubia Gardens
PARK

2 ⊙ Map p28, A4

Stretching out behind the Koutoubia Mosque, this palm-tree-dotted swath of greenery is a Marrakshi favourite spot for strolling, relaxing on park benches and for generally taking a quiet break. If you need some downtime after dodging motorbikes amid the medina's skinny alleyways, take the locals' lead and head here for a peaceful meander. There are great views of Koutoubia Mosque's minaret to be enjoyed. (Ave Mohammed V; ⊙8am-8pm)

Understand
How to Dress

In the ville nouvelle shorts and singlets (tank tops) are fine, but in the medina, where life remains more traditional, your choice of attire may be perceived as a sign of respect for yourself and Moroccans alike. For both men and women this means not wearing shorts, sleeveless tops or revealing clothing. If you do, some people will be embarrassed for you and the family that raised you and will avoid eye contact. So if you don't want to miss out on some excellent company – especially among older Moroccans – dress modestly.

Medina Spa HAMMAM

 3 Map p28, E2

Enjoy a brisk scrubbing and rejuvenating steam just steps from the dusty Djemaa, off Rue des Banques. This is a busy riad-spa, so expect some noise, line-dry and maybe damp (though clean) robes, and waits for walk-ins. (📞0524 38 50 59; www.medina-spa-marrakech.com; 27 Derb Zaari; hammam & gommage from Dh150; ⏰9.30am-9pm)

Koubba of Fatima Zohra TOMB

 4 Map p28, A3

The plain-white modest structure that sits near the Koutoubia Mosque (p26) is the tomb of Fatima Zohra, daughter of a revered local religious leader. Local legends abound about Fatima Zohra's mystical powers, but the most popular story is that she would turn into a dove every evening and only resume human form at sunrise. (Ave Mohammed V)

Eating

Djemaa el-Fna Food Stalls MOROCCAN $

 5 Map p28, C2

Grilled meat and tajines as far as the eye can see! Plus Moroccan specialities of snail soup, sheep's brains and skewered hearts for the more adventurous gourmands. Eating amid the mayhem of the Djemaa food stalls at least once in your trip is not to be missed. Always go for the busiest stalls as they'll have the freshest meat. (mains Dh30-50; ⏰sunset-1am)

Le Tobsil MOROCCAN $$$

 6 Map p28, B2

In this intimate riad near Bab Laksour, 50 guests (max) indulge in button-popping, five-course Moroccan menus with aperitifs and wine pairings, as Gnaoua musicians strum quietly in the courtyard. Don't let the belly dancers distract you from your salads, *pastilla* (savoury-sweet pie), tajines and couscous, capped with mint tea, fruit and Moroccan pastries. Booking required. (📞0524 44 40 52; 22 Derb Abdellah ben Hessaien; 5-course menu incl wine Dh640, ⏱7.30-11pm Wed-Mon)

Hadj Mustapha
MOROCCAN $

7 🍴 Map p28, D2

Several stalls at Souq Ablueh offer up paper-sealed crockpots of *tanjia*, but Hadj Mustapha's is the most renowned for sampling this famed 'bachelor's stew', with basic but clean seating inside a well-scuffed stall. Use bread as your utensil to scoop up *tanjia*, sprinkled with cumin and salt, and chase with olives. (Souq Ablueh, east side; tanjia with bread & olives Dh70; ⏱noon-8pm)

Gastro MK
MEDITERRANEAN $$$

8 🍴 Map p28, B1

This place has been causing quite the stir in foodie circles since it swung open its riad doors for dinner guests. Chef Omar El Ouahssoussi blends both Moroccan and French influences to serve up a menu that's a treat for Moroccan cuisine newbies as well as more well-travelled tongues. Seats just 20 people per night; advance booking is a must. (📞0524 37 61 73; www.maison mk.com; 14 Derb Sebaai; 5-course tasting menu Dh640; ⏱Thu-Tue from 7.30pm)

Marrakech Henna Art Cafe
CAFE $

9 🍴 Map p28, D4

This charming cafe and art space is a cosy retreat dishing up a mixed menu

of North African (the Berber omelette and turkey *brochettes* (kebabs) with caramelised pumpkin are winners) and healthy-leaning sandwiches. True to its name there are local art exhibits, a collection of Berber artefacts, wall murals and the opportunity to get your own piece of henna body art. (📞0524 38 14 10; www.marrakechhenna artcafe.com; 35 Derb Siquya; mains Dh40; ⏱10am-9pm; ⏱ 🛜 📷)

Roti d'Or
INTERNATIONAL $

10 🍴 Map p28, E2

Blink and you'd miss it, but Roti d'Or is not a place to miss if you're looking for a good-value non-Moroccan meal in the medina. Enchiladas, a Tex-Mex burger and felafel sandwiches feature on the menu, all served with a tangy rice salad and chips. (Kennaria Dabbachi; mains Dh25-40; ⏱10.30am-9pm)

Ⓠ Local Life
Mechoui Alley

Just before noon, the vendors at this row of **stalls** (Map p28, D2; Souq Ablueh, east side; mechoui Dh50-70; ⏱11am-2pm) start carving up steaming sides of *mechoui* (slow-roasted lamb). Point to the best-looking cut of meat, and ask for a *nuss* (half) or *rubb* (quarter) kilo. The cook will hack off falling-from-the-bone lamb and hand it to you with fresh-baked bread, cumin, salt and olives.

Kafé Fnaque Berbère   CAFE $

11 ✗ Map p28, C1

If we're not strolling Djemaa el-Fna at sunset, we're admiring the sky turning red over the medina rooftops on the dinkiest terrace in Marrakesh. Dig into the hummus or feast on a home-style tangy *tanjia*. It's above a teeny bookshop with some good coffee-table books on Marrakesh. (☏0649 58 31 65; Rue Laksour; mains Dh35-75; ☺10am-9pm; 🛜)

Earth Café   VEGETARIAN $$

12 ✗ Map p28, E4

Now for something completely different. The Earth Café, right in the heart of the souqs, is small, but its veggie culinary ambitions are great.

You'll have no problem getting your five-plus a day here with your choice of burgers and stir-fry-style dishes as well as freshly squeezed fruit and veg smoothies. Vegan options available too. (☏0661 28 94 02; 2 Derb Zouak; mains Dh70; ☺11am-11pm; 🛜🍴)

Pâtisserie des Princes   PASTRIES $

13 ✗ Map p28, C4

This is one of the city's most famous patisseries, with enough *pain au chocolat*, petits fours, almond cookies and ice cream to keep Djemaa el-fna dentists in business. The small cafe at the back is a welcome respite for women, or anyone in search of a quiet pot of tea. (☏0524 44 30 33; 32 Rue Bab Agnaou; ☺9am-9pm; 🍴❄)

Intricate henna hand tattoos

EMILY MARIE WILSON/SHUTTERSTOCK ©

Café Kessabine
MOROCCAN $$

14 Map p28, E2

Snuggled right in the far corner of Djemaa el-Fna, the Kessabine may not have the panoramic views across the plaza that other restaurants can claim, but it makes up for that with a chilled-out, slightly bohemian vibe and friendly (although painfully slow) service. Nosh out on a menu of tajines, *pastilla* and salads. (0665 29 37 96; 77 Souq Quessabine; dishes Dh35-80; 9am-11pm)

Oscar Progrès
MOROCCAN $

15 Map p28, C4

This brightly lit local canteen serves up huge plates of couscous and sizzling *brochettes* to hungry office workers who take a pew at long com munal tables. Despite the dining-hall atmosphere, the food is of a good standard and the service efficient and pleasant. (20 Rue Bani Marine; mains Dh35-45; noon-11pm;)

El Bahja
MOROCCAN $

16 Map p28, C4

Serving up filling portions of *kefta* (meatballs) and Moroccan staples to a steady stream of hungry local workers and travellers, El Bahja is a stalwart of the Djemaa el-Fna scene. The food here isn't going to knock your socks off, but it's always dependable, good value and fresh. (0524 44 13 51; 24 Rue Bani Marine; mains Dh35-45; noon-11pm)

Drinking

Café de France
CAFE

17 Map p28, D2

Djemaa old-timer Cafe de France is still one of the best places on the square to put your feet up and watch the world go by. Join the regulars on the front terrace and order a *nus-nus* (half coffee, half milk) or head upstairs to the balconies for good views across the square. Serves up decent breakfasts as well for Dh35 to Dh45. (Djemaa el-Fna; 8am-10pm)

Local Life
Henna Tattoos

Natural henna dye – extracted from the dried leaves of the henna tree – is applied traditionally during celebrations, particularly on the Islamic festival of Eid al-Adha and before wedding ceremonies when the women gather together to adorn the bride-to-be. Henna tattoo artists hang out on Djemaa el-Fna. Be careful, though: some may use 'black henna', which can contain chemicals known to cause skin allergies, rather than natural henna, which is a reddish brown. **Henna Cafe** (Map p44, B2; www.henna cafemarrakech.com; 93 Arset Aouzal; tattoos from Dh50; 11am-8pm;) and Marrakech Henna Art Cafe (p31) both have henna artists on hand and guarantee they use natural henna.

Café des Souks
CAFE

18 Map p28, D1

This old-fashioned cafe is hidden right inside bustling Rue Semmarine and makes a good pit-stop for tea or a cold drink. It also does excellent *beghrir* (Moroccan pancakes) for breakfast. (Souq Semmarine; ⊙8am-4pm)

Piano Bar
BAR

19 Map p28, B2

Step from the red Berber carpet into the classiest gin joint in the medina. Powerful long drinks (Dh70 to Dh90) are delivered to leather club chairs as jazz classics soar to cedar ceilings. A second plush seating area behind the pool makes a serene escape for non-smokers and jazz-avoiders, and the terrace restaurant serves a decent Indian curry. (☎0524 38 88 00; www.lesjardinsdela koutoubia.com; Les Jardins de la Koutoubia, 26 Rue el-Koutoubia; ⊙5pm-1am)

Top Tip

Getting Cash in the Medina

No, you don't need to troop all the way to the ville nouvelle to find an ATM *(guichets automatiques)*. There are ATMs on Rue Bab Agnaou (which runs off Djemaa el-Fna) and also near Place Rahba Kedima. Time your cashflow so you don't need to top up funds on a Sunday when the medina ATMs tend to be empty of cash.

Café el Koutoubia
CAFE

20 Map p28, B3

The street-side terrace at this charmingly old-fashioned cafe has cracking views of the Koutoubia Minaret just across the road. It's a favourite hang-out for both elderly jellaba-clad gentlemen and suited businesspeople catching up on a work break which, despite its prime position, gives it a properly local ambience. (Ave Mohammed V; ⊙8.30am-10pm)

Bakchich
CAFE

21 Map p28, E2

This laid-back spot is a good choice after weaving through the souqs. Grab one of the tables decorated with labels from tinned sardines and tinned fruit that rim the front entrance; order a juice and watch the alley traffic pass by. There's a decent menu of tajines and sandwiches (Dh30 to Dh55) if you're feeling peckish. (Kennaria Dabachi; ⊙10.30am-11pm)

Riad Yima
TEAHOUSE

22 Map p28, D1

Acclaimed Marrakshi artist and photographer Hassan Hajjaj created this kitsch-crammed tearoom and gallery. Preconceived notions of Moroccan restaurants and riads, with their Arabian Nights fantasy of candlelit lanterns, arches and belly dancers, are revamped with a tongue-in-cheek humour, accompanied by a traditional glass of mint tea, of course. (☎0524 39 19 87; www.riadyima.com; 52 Derb Aarjane, Rahba Kedima; ⊙9am-6pm Mon-Sat; 🛜)

Understand

Storytellers & Tall Tales

The Original Smooth Talkers

Marrakesh has a strong tradition of *hikayat* (oral storytelling). For centuries, history soaked in myth, fictional ancient epics of heroic derring-do and morality tales have been passed down through the generations by storytellers whose narrative skills were highly prized and sought-after. This popular art form was not just for entertainment. It was a vital tool for passing on knowledge about the wider world. Storytellers regaled eager listeners with tales from the great Arab classic *The Thousand and One Nights*, narrated the lives of *marabouts* (saints), spun Moroccan folk tales and fables, and told wondrous and terrible stories of faraway travel and adventure. Djemaa el-Fna is thought to have been firmly established as a central platform for storytellers to wow the crowds by the 11th century. It is because of this age-old tradition that Unesco declared the Djemaa el-Fna a 'Masterpiece of World Heritage' in 2001.

An Endangered Ancient Craft

Today though, there are fewer and fewer storytellers. In the 20th century the advent of radio, television and finally the internet has eroded their once-important role. Where the magical stories of the greater world were brought to life by the storyteller's tales, now news and entertainment arrives on a small screen. Djemaa el-Fna's traditional storytellers, who spent years learning their craft through digesting ancient tales, are all either nearing retirement or already retired. The city's famed square is now a hub for far more boisterous performances and musical acts.

A New Generation

Recently there has been a resurgent interest in saving *hikayat* from extinction. A project at Cafe Clock (p91) has partnered a famed Djemaa storyteller with a group of young local apprentices who perform the tales he spins in English, bringing the rich art of Moroccan storytelling to a wider audience. There is a future for Marrakesh's storytellers after all.

Café du Grand Balcon
CAFE

23 Map p28, D3

Yes it's a total tourist trap, but the roof terrace here is *the* place on the Djemaa to get a good overall view of the carnival of life below. Head straight upstairs, buy a drink (you can't enter without buying something) and get your camera ready for panoramic plaza views. (Djemaa el-Fna; ⏰8am-11pm)

Chez Chegrouni
CAFE

24 Map p28, E2

It's all about the terrace views over the square at Chez Chegrouni. Nab a table at the front and you've scored prime Djemaa-watching territory. There's a menu of classic tajine options for the hungry, though it's better for just a drink can be hit and miss. (Djemaa el-Fna; ⏰8am-11pm)

Le Marrakchi
CAFE

25 Map p28, D2

Grab one of the window tables so you've got ringside seats high above the Djemaa action. This is one of the few restaurants serving alcohol around the square, and cheerful staff

 Local Life
Juice on the Djemaa
Get your vitamin C fix the local way by slurping down a freshly squeezed orange juice for Dh4 at one of the orange juice stalls on Djemaa el-Fna.

seem happy for punters to pop in just for a drink. Bear in mind that a cheesy belly-dancing performance may break out while you're there. (☎0524 44 33 77; Rue des Banques; ⏰noon-midnight)

Taj'in Darna
CAFE

26 Map p28, D3

If it's time to put your feet up after entering into some Djemaa action, Taj'in Darna is a relaxed haven on the square's rim – just the ticket for a cold-drink stop or your umpteenth mint tea. If it's views you're after, head up the rickety stairs to the large, shady terrace. (☎0670 21 31 91; 50 Djemaa el-Fna; ⏰9.30am-11pm)

Le Salama
BAR

27 Map p28, E2

The food isn't great and the evening belly-dancing show is more cringe-inducing than razzle-dazzle, but skip all that and head to the rooftop for a sunset beer or bottle of wine. This is one of the few places near the square where you can enjoy a sundowner, plus it has a happy hour with two-for-one beers (usually from about 5pm). (☎0524 39 13 00; www.lesalama.com; 40 Rue des Banques; ⏰11am-midnight)

Hôtel Islane
CAFE

28 Map p28, B3

The menu may be so-so at best but this hotel has snaffled top position across the road from the Koutoubia Mosque. Stop in for a coffee, pot of tea, or beer on the rooftop terrace for

Attracting customers at a Djemaa el-Fna food stall (p30)

superb views of the minaret. (📞0524 440 081; Ave Mohammed V; ⊗8am-10pm)

Shopping

Al Nour   ARTS & CRAFTS

 29 Map p28, B1

A smart cooperative run by local women with disabilities where you can find household linens minutely embroidered along the edges. You can also get fabulous hand-stitched Marrakesh-mod tunics, dresses and shirts for men, women and kids, and there's no extra charge for alterations. Purchases pay for salaries, training programs and a childcare centre.

(📞0524 39 03 23; www.alnour-textiles.com; Rue Laksour 57; ⊗9am-2pm & 3-7pm Sat-Wed)

Fondouq el Ouarzazi   ARTS & CRAFTS

30 Map p28, C2

This slightly decrepit *fondouq* (rooming house) is a dream come true for shoppers who enjoy poking about in pursuit of the perfect find as much as the actual buying. Several cubby-hole shops have claimed space on the upper balcony and are a clutter of traditional jewellery, Berber artefacts and dusty antiques. Accept a mint tea from the shopkeepers and hunt away. (Pl Bab Fteuh; ⊗10am-6pm)

Understand
The Making of Marrakesh

The Berber Sanhaja tribe founded the Almoravid dynasty in the 11th century and swept through the south of Morocco, demolishing opponents as they rode north. They pitched their campsite on a desolate swath of land that would become Marrakesh.

Almoravid Berber leader Youssef ben Tachfine and his savvy wife Zeinab recognised its strategic potential, and built ramparts around the encampment in AD 1062. The Almoravids established the city's *khettara* (underground irrigation canals) and signature pink mudbrick architecture.

At the age of almost 80, Youssef ben Tachfine launched successful campaigns securing Almoravid control of Andalucia. Marrakesh, once just a patch of dirt, became the operational centre of an empire that stretched right up to Barcelona's city limits.

Art Ouarzazate
FASHION & ACCESSORIES

31 🔒 Map p28, E1

Tried and tested techniques in weaving, leather work and embroidery are transformed into high-fashion dandy jackets, sari-grafted coats and wire-rimmed 'papillon' dresses by dynamic duo Samad and Malek. Beyond the clothes racks there are also bags, *babouches* (leather slippers) and quirky poufs and cushions for sale. (📞0648 58 48 33; 15 Zinkat Rahba; ⊙9am-8pm)

Souq Ableuh
FOOD

32 🔒 Map p28, D2

Swerve off Djemaa el-Fna to this tiny souq dedicated to olives: green, black, purple, marinated in spicy *harissa* paste... It's basically olive heaven. (Souq Ableuh)

Kif-Kif
ARTS & CRAFTS

33 🔒 Map p28, B1

A hip boutique near Bab Ksour that engages the city's most inventive artisans to come up with clever gifts: handbags woven from recycled T-shirts, rings with interchangeable felt baubles, and adorable children's nightgowns embroidered with 'good night' in Arabic. Ten percent of the price on all kids' items goes to a local nonprofit children's organisation. (📞0661 08 20 41; www.kifkifbystef.com; 8 Rue Laksour; ⊙9am-9pm)

Warda La Mouche
FASHION & ACCESSORIES

34 🔒 Map p28, E3

Those after a touch of Moroccan boho-chic style should definitely have a fossick through the clothes racks

Tajines on display near Djemaa el-Fna

here. Floaty sundresses with quirky embroidery detail, summery tops with post-hippie flair and sophisticated harem-pant styles await to be snapped up for your suitcase. The kid's clothing range is pretty adorable, too. (📞0524 38 90 63; 127 Kennaria Dabachi; ⏰10am-6pm)

Ouarzazate Huiles Essentielles
COSMETICS

35 🔒 Map p28, E3

This sweet-smelling shop with its range of argan, cactus, jasmine and amber skincare oils and creams solves your gift problems for those hard-to-buy-for friends or relatives in your life. The women working here can also demonstrate the hard work involved in making argan oil by grinding the heavy chunks of argan. (📞0524 42 73 54; 1 Kennaria Debachi; ⏰9.30am-6pm)

Pâtisserie Dounia
FOOD & DRINKS

36 🔒 Map p28, D1

Sweet tooth treats ahoy. The traditional Moroccan delicacies here are all about sesame, almond and sticky syrup, and make a great gift for gourmet friends (if you manage to resist eating them yourself). (Souq Semmarine; ⏰10am-6.30pm)

Explore

Mouassine &
Bab Doukkala

Mouassine is a showcase of the medina's changing face. While narrow slivers of traditional souqs are still piled high with twinkling lamps and rainbow stripes of leatherware, a fresh breed of boutiques and lounge-style cafes are also making their mark. Traditionalists shouldn't fret though: donkey-cart action and crumbling *fondouq* (rooming house) architecture continues to rule in Mouassine.

The Sights in a Day

Begin a morning in Mouassine by contemplating the rich decoration of **Musée de Mouassine** (p45) then move on to Rue Dar el-Bacha to discover Marrakesh's best remnants of its caravan-city heritage. This stretch is home to some of the medina's most interesting *fondouqs*.

Linger over lunch in the leafy courtyard at **Le Jardin** (p51) then indulge in a spot of souvenir hunting with a wander through the souqs. Exploring the maze-like lanes around here can leave you feeling a little worn and dusty, so either hop along to **Hammam Mouassine** (p46) for some steam relief or relax amid the rejuvenated riad gardens of **Le Jardin Secret** (p45). Afterwards, go for a mint tea at **Dar Cherifa** (p52); it's not often you get to take a tea break surrounded by stunning Saadian era architecture.

Dining within the medina is all about rooftops and riads. Choose the rooftop and head to **Souk Kafé** (p50) for lip-smacking *mezze* (salads) and aromatic tajines. Finish off the evening with a cocktail at **Café Arabe** (p52).

For a local's day in Bab Doukkala, see p42.

Local Life

Bab Doukkala Neighbourhood Stroll (p42)

 Best of Marrakesh

Food

La Maison Arabe (p50)

Latitude 31 (p51)

Spas & Hammams

Hammam Mouassine (p46)

Le Bain Bleu (p47)

Heritage Spa (p47)

Hammam de la Rose (p48)

Hammam Dar el-Bacha (p50)

Hammam Bab Doukkala (p50)

Gardens

Le Jardin Secret (p45)

Getting There

Walk From Djemaa el-Fna, head west on Souq Quessabine until you reach Pl Bab Fteuh. Turn onto Rue Mouassine and head straight up to the Mouassine Mosque.

Taxi Taxis can drop you at Bab Doukkala or on Rue Dar el-Glaoui, close to the palace of Dar el-Bacha; a useful option if you don't want to walk far.

Local Life
Bab Doukkala Neighbourhood Stroll

If you thought the medina was all about shopping for shiny things, you thought wrong. If you've had your fill of haggling (or your suitcase is already stuffed to the brim full of new finds), head to the Bab Doukkala area to explore a quieter, more residential, part of this old city.

❶ Enter Through Bab Doukkala

The grand gate of **Bab Doukkala** (Rue Bab Doukkala) is definitely looking down-at-heel today, but this horseshoe-arched entryway once guarded Marrakesh's northwest walls. Head through the tower arch and down the bustling local market street of **Rue Bab Doukkala** where carcasses swing from butcher's hooks, stalls display fresh fish, and fruit carts are laden with oranges.

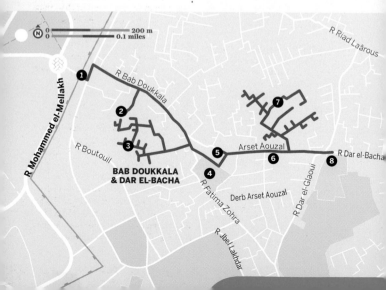

2 Stroll Tranquil Derb Essamour

The narrow dead-end alleyway of **Derb Essamour** is well worth a wander for the photogenic effect of the peeling plasterwork on the walls. In particular check out the gorgeous old door of house number 11.

3 Get Lost In Derb Dekah

Derb Dekah is a vast alley network and nearly completely residential. Here, washing hangs from iron window-grills, pot plants spruce up painted doorways and the only pedestrians you'll meet are homemakers toting shopping. Don't worry if you think you're getting lost. Every turn is a dead end so all you have to do is double-back.

4 Around Bab Doukkala Mosque

The **Bab Doukkala Mosque** (Rue Fatima Zohra; ☉closed to non-Muslims) sits beside a small square, its minaret towering above the palm trees. The local plaza is always a hive of activity, rimmed by cubby-hole food stands with sizzling grills. It's a hang-out point for delivery-cart folk catching a break in the shade.

5 Doukkala Fountain

Swing by the furniture-maker workshops on the mosque's north side to arrive at the **Doukkala Fountain**. Before water was pumped into medina housing, public fountains played a major role in local lives. Although

now dry, and rather decrepit, it still bears an intricate lintel. For a close-up, squeeze past the parked cars into the fenced-off area.

6 Henna Cafe Break

Take a break at friendly **Henna Cafe** (www.hennacafemarrakech.com; 93 Arset Aouzal; ☉Dh40, tattoos from Dh50; ☉11am-8pm; 🛜🍴), where you can munch on a tasty *kefta* (meatball) sandwich while getting an intricate hand or foot henna decoration from the resident *nquasha* (henna artist). For a further feel-good factor, all profits here go to local residents in need.

7 Wander Through Derb el Halfaoui

Although the riad guesthouses have begun to move in, much of this maze of back lanes is quiet and residential. **Derb el Halfaoui** has a closed-in ambience, with plenty of dimly lit, low passageways separating narrow streets, where the sky is reduced to a mere sliver of blue above.

8 At the Pasha's Palace

End your stroll at **Dar el-Bacha Palace** (Rue Dar el-Bacha), once the home of Marrakesh's feared pasha, Thami El-Glaoui, governor during Morocco's French protectorate era. Gaze up at the grand facade (the building is closed to visitors) and imagine the power El-Glaoui wielded – hob-nobbing with Churchill and Eisenhower one minute, then issuing mafia-style executions the next.

RIAD LAÂROUS

BAB DOUKKALA & DAR EL-BACHA

MOUASSINE

For reviews see

◎ Sights	p45
✕ Eating	p50
🍷 Drinking	p52
🛍 Shopping	p55

R Amesfah
R Riad el-Arous
R Riad Laârous
R Riad el-Arous
Zawiya Sidi Abd el-Aziz
Fondouq Kharbouch
Fondouq el-Amir
Souq Krhachbia
Souq des Teinturiers
Souq Lebbadine
Le Jardin Secret
Bradia El Kedima
Mousassine
Mouassine Fountain
Mouassine Mosque
Musée de Mouassine
Hammam Mouassine
Derb Chorfa Lakbir
Le Bain Bleu
R Sidi el-Yamani
R Laksour
R Mouassine
Hammam de la Rose
Derb Tizeguarine
R Dar el-Bacha
R Dar el-Giaoui
Heritage Spa
Arset Aouzal
Derb Arset Aouzal
Bab Doukkala Mosque
Derb Zaouia
Derb Assehbe
R Fatima Zohra
R Jbel Lakhdar
R Bab Doukkala

200 m
0.1 miles

Colourful dyed wool, Souq des Teinturiers (p46)

Sights

Musée de Mouassine   MUSEUM

1  Map p44, E4

House-hunting in the medina, Patrick Menac'h stumbled across a historic treasure of great cultural significance. Beneath the layers of white plaster of a modest riad's 1st-floor *douiria* (guest apartment) was a jewel of domestic Saadian architecture, c 1560. The riad's ground-floor rooms hold a small collection of Berber artefacts, but the painstakingly restored interior of the upstairs salons, with their intricate cornice friezes and painted woodwork, are the true star of this charming museum. (☎0524 38 57 21; www.museede mouassine.com; 5 Derb el Hammam; Dh30; ⏱9.30am-7pm)

Le Jardin Secret   MUSEUM

2  Map p44, E3

Take a souq time-out to enjoy a traditional medina garden revived for the 21st century. This historic riad was once owned by powerful *caïd* (local chief) U-Bihi, who was poisoned by Mohammed IV. The palatial grounds comprise both an exotic and traditional Islamic garden fed by a restored original *khettara* underground irrigation system, a pavilion with exhibits on the riad's history (including a fascinating documentary on the restoration process), a cafe, and a tower with views

Understand
The Architecture of Musée de Mouassine

The Saadians lavished mighty building projects on Marrakesh, transforming the city into their capital. All the surviving architecture of their reign – the mosques at Mouassine, Bab Doukkala, Ben-Youssef and Sidi Bel-Abbes – are grand in scale, which makes Mouassine's bijou *douiria* (guest apartment), now open to the public as the Museé de Mouassine (p45), a significantly rare architectural example from this period. The *douiria* was no imperial project. It was created by a *chorfa* (noble) family after the Saadians relocated the Mouassine Jews to the *mellah* (Jewish quarter) and gave the city a new dynamic. The *douiria* in its restored form allows us to imagine the lifestyle of a noble family during the Saadian reign and is an important commentary on the courtly art of hospitality during this era.

The main salon is a symphony of colour, while bedrooms are trimmed with sculpted Kufic script framed by azure blue and finished with Pompeian red skirting. You may assume the vivid colours on show are the work of the 24-person restoration team but the decor is, amazingly, original – preserved beneath layers of plaster for centuries.

across the medina. (☎0524 39 00 40; www.lejardinsecretmarrakech.com; 121 Rue Mouassine; adult/child Dh50/free; tower adult/child Dh30/20; ☺10.30am-7pm)

Souq des Teinturiers SOUQ

3 ◉ Map p44, E3

The dyers' souq is one of Marrakesh's most colourful market sights. Here you'll find skeins of coloured wool draped from the rafters and a rainbow of colour pigment pots outside the stalls. (Souq des Teinturiers; ☺irregular hours)

Hammam Mouassine HAMMAM

4 ◉ Map p44, E3

A proper public hammam that also caters for travellers looking for an authentic experience. In business since 1562, Hammam Mouassine has charming and professional staff to wash and then scrub you down with Morocco's famed rhassoul clay until you're squeaky clean. As it's a public hammam, you could also choose to DIY it here for just Dh10 entrance fee. (Derb el-Hammam; hammam & gommage Dh100; ☺5am-midnight)

Fondouq el-Amir HISTORIC BUILDING

5 ◉ Map p44, D2

This well-preserved *fondouq* would have once been the staging post for medieval merchants doing business in the city, but today the courtyard chambers are filled with small artisan shops. It's particularly noteworthy for the red ochre geometric decoration of diamonds, hexagons and stars that borders its internal stone arches. (Rue Dar el-Bacha)

Fondouq Kharbouch

HISTORIC BUILDING

6 ◉ Map p44, E2

The inner courtyard of this *fondouq* may now be home to a ramshackle collection of workshops, with power lines strung precariously between windows, but the spacious grace and pleasing proportions of this old merchant inn haven't been lost. The upper balconies still cling to threads of wooden ceilings now supported by plain white plaster pillars. (Rue Dar el-Bacha)

Le Bain Bleu

HAMMAM

7 ◉ Map p44, D4

Top-notch pampering awaits. Follow the signs for Dar Cherifa off Rue el-Mouassine onto Derb Chorfa Lakbir, where this riad spa-hammam features secluded patios, sleek subterranean steam rooms and professional treatments to soothe the souq-weary. Couples hammam packages, plus facials, manicures and pedicures available. (☏0524 38 38 04; www.lebainbleu. com; 32 Derb Chorfa Lakbir; hammam & gommage Dh200, with massage from Dh600; ◷10am-11pm)

Heritage Spa

HAMMAM

8 ◉ Map p44, B2

Forget any illusions of authentically local hammams and bliss out in this private spa-hammam with a deep-cleansing sea salt exfoliation (Dh300) or a detoxing black-soap and bitter-orange scrub (Dh290). Afterwards, stressed travellers can soothe jet-lagged skin with a pampering massage using essential oils (from Dh450). (☏0524 38 43 33; www.heritagesparmar rakech.com; 40 Derb Arset Aouzal; hammam & gommage from Dh290; ◷10am-8pm)

Mouassine Fountain

FOUNTAIN

9 ◉ Map p44, E3

The medina had 80 fountains at the start of the 20th century; each neighbourhood had its own for water for

Top Tip

Keep to the Right

Sure, those zippy motorbikes and unwieldy donkey-led rubbish collecting carts can be annoying when you're walking through the medina's lanes. Remember, though, this is a living city, not a museum, and the people who live and work here need to be able to get around. You are far less likely to find yourself dodging carts and bikes if you try to keep to the right while walking through the alleys. And always keep alert for two-wheeled traffic coming up behind you.

Mouassine Fountain's intricately carved wooden lintel (p47)

cooking, public baths, orchards and gardens. The Mouassine Fountain, near Rue el-Mouassine, is a prime example, with carved wood details and continued use as a neighbourhood wool-drying area and gossip source. (Souq Lebbadine)

Hammam de la Rose HAMMAM

10 ⦿ Map p44, D2

This private hammam gets the thumbs-up for its super-professional staff and squeaky-clean premises. There's a range of beauty treatments you can add, from rose facial masks and clay cleansing to a host of massage options. (☎0524 44 47 69; www. hammamdelarose.com; 130 Rue Dar el-Bacha; hammam & gommage Dh250; ⊙10am-8pm)

Zawiya Sidi Abd el-Aziz SHRINE

11 ⦿ Map p44, E2

On the corner where Rue Amesfah splits, note the door with stained glass and plasterwork detailing that sits snug in the high alley wall. This is the entry to the Zawiya Sidi Abd el-Aziz religious complex, a shrine honouring one of Marrakesh's seven saints. (Rue Riad Laârous; ⊙closed to non-Muslims)

Zawiya Sidi Ben-Slimane SHRINE

12 ⦿ Map p44, D1

This is the shrine of Sheik al-Jazuli, author of the *Dala'il al-Kharat* (Guide to Goodness). (Rue Sidi Ben-Slimane; ⊙closed to non-Muslims)

Understand

Hammam Etiquette

Rub-a-dub-dub. Marrakesh is the perfect place to tick off the hammam experience, whether you want to scrub away the alley dust in a public hammam or reward yourself with a treat at a private spa-style hammam. Whichever you choose, expect a vigorous *gommage* (scrub-down by an attendant) that leaves you rejuvenated – and with half your epidermis flaked away.

In past centuries hammams were the only source of hot water in the medina. Traditionally they are built of mudbrick, lined with *tadelakt* (satiny, hand-polished limestone plaster that traps moisture) and capped with a dome that has star-shaped vents to let steam escape.

Public Hammams

If you're up for local interaction and a bit of an adventure, the public hammam is the way to go. You'll need a hammam kit of towel, flip-flops and a plastic mat (to sit on), as well as a spare pair of underwear and your shampoo and soap.

In public hammams no one bathes entirely nude. Both men and women keep their underpants on. In some female hammams knickers and bra are the norm, while in others only knickers are usually worn. However, it's always perfectly acceptable to wear something on top. Wearing your swimsuit is also fine.

Some public hammams are unmarked and others simply have a picture of a man or woman stencilled on the wall outside. Ask a local for hammam recommendations. At all hammams sexes are segregated and there's usually separate bathing times for men and women.

Private Hammams

Marrakesh's private hammams are more like spas, with the most luxurious of them offering a range of add-on beauty treatments. You don't need to bring anything along; it's all provided, usually including a nifty pair of paper knickers to wear. It's also perfectly acceptable to wear your own swimsuit.

Local Life

Public Hammams

If you want the true-blue hammam experience with all the locals, rather than the one polished up for the tourists, grab your hammam bag (kit yourself out with scrubbing mitts and other bathing essentials at shops within the souqs) and swing on by to either of these public hammams.

Marrakesh's largest traditional hammam, **Hammam Dar el-Bacha** (Map 44, B4; 20 Rue Fatima Zohra; Dh10; ◷ men 7am-1pm, women 1-9pm) has star-shaped vents in the vast domed ceiling.

A historic hammam, dating from the 17th century, **Hammam Bab Doukkala** (Map 44, B2; Rue Bab Doukkala; Dh10; ◷ women noon-7pm, men from 8pm) is in the southeast corner of Bab Doukkala Mosque. It has heated *tadelakt* (polished plaster) floors and a mellow atmosphere during men's hours.

Eating

Souk Kafé   MOROCCAN $$

13 Map p44, E2

Pull up a hand-hewn stool under terrace parasols and stay a while: this is authentic local food worth savouring. The Moroccan *mezze* of six cooked vegetable dishes qualifies as lunch for two, and the vegetarian Berber couscous is surprisingly hearty – but wait until you get a whiff of the aromatic Marrakshi *tanjia,* with its slow-cooked, perfectly falling apart beef. (☏0662 61 02 29; 11 Derb Sidi Abdelaziz; mains Dh90-120; ◷9am-9pm; ❋ 🛜)

La Maison Arabe   MOROCCAN $$$

14 Map p44, A3

La Maison Arabe was serving Moroccan fine dining decades before other riads, and *viva la différence!* The focus here is on the food and service, with excellent classical Andalucian musicians providing subtle background music for traditional tajine and couscous feasts. Make an evening of it and drop into the piano bar for an apéritif before your meal. (☏0524 38 70 10; www.lamaisonarabe.com; 1 Derb Assehbe; mains Dh150-200; ◷7.30pm-midnight; 🛜 🍴)

La Table du Palais   MEDITERRANEAN $$$

15 Map p44, D3

Nothing beats a palm-shaded lunch after a morning haggling in the souqs; this tranquil courtyard restaurant delivers on peaceful ambience. The menus cherry-pick French and Moroccan influences with ease, creating a Mediterranean fusion. If you come for dinner (bookings recommended), pop into the jazzy little bar for a nightcap before you leave. (☏0524 38 50 55; www.palaislamrani.com; Riad Palais Lamrani, 63 Rue Sidi el-Yamani; plate of the day Dh150, set menus Dh220-250; ◷noon-2.30pm Mon-Sat, 7.30-9.30pm Fri & Sat; 🛜)

Beats Burger BURGERS $$

16 Map p44, E2

No, we didn't expect to find a gourmet burger joint sitting snug amid the souqs either. Sign of the times indeed. If you're tajined-out for the day, hit this place for burgers with a difference – stuffed with hash browns, *harissa* mayonnaise and duck breast – or keep your health halo glowing with a vegan bagel. (📱0524 39 12 13; www.beatsburger. com; 35 Souq Jeld Kemakine; mains Dh55-115; ⏱11am-9pm; 🛜🍽)

Le Jardin MOROCCAN $$

17 Map p44, E2

Entrepreneur Kamal Laftimi transformed this 17th-century riad in the medina's core into a tranquil oasis where you can lunch beneath a canopy of banana trees, serenaded by songbirds, as tiny tortoises inch across the floor tiles. The menu can be hit and miss, but shines with its big-portioned *brochettes* (kebabs) and whole grilled sardines. (📱0524 37 82 95; www.lejardin.ma; 32 Derb Sidi Abdelaziz; mains Dh80-140; 🛜🍽)

Kui-Zin INTERNATIONAL $$

18 Map p44, E1

As you're munching on complimentary olives and fresh-baked bread, choose from a menu that spins from couscous and tajines to vegetable lasagne (actually a delicious, cheesy carrot and courgette pie) and chicken curry. Chef Kenza takes real pride in the preparation, while Hassan serves everything with a heartfelt smile. Come for dinner and get live music thrown in, too. (📱0524 00 09 04, www. kui-zin.com; 12 Rue Amesfah; mains Dh50-90; ⏱11am-10pm Tue-Sun; 🛜🍽)

Terrasse des Épices MOROCCAN $$

19 Map p44, E2

Follow the basket bubble-lamps to lunch on top of the souqs in a mud-brick *bhou* (booth) off Rue Dar el-Bacha for a dining ambience of hazy, lazy Mediterranean days. Put on your monogrammed sunhat and pick a tajine from the Moroccan menu or go global with

Local Life
Foodie Finds on Rue el-Giza

Scruffy Rue el-Giza (which runs west off Rue Riad Laârous) is the unlikely home of two foodie treats. **Babouche Café** (📱0675 36 94 68; Rue el-Giza; mains Dh25-55; ⏱11.30am-11.30pm Mon-Sat; 🛜) is a hole-in-the-wall cafe neighbouring a car park; it dishes up some of the tastiest cheap tajines in the medina. At **Latitude 31** (📱0524 38 49 34; www. latitude31marrakech.com; 186 Rue el Giza; mains Dh130-210; ⏱6-11pm; 🛜) traditional cuisines are tweaked without raising eyebrows, pretty much pulling off a Moroccan-fusion menu. Not all dishes completely gel but its take on *mrouzia* (lamb tajine with honey, raisins and almonds) is a sweet-sticky-savoury delight.

Top Tip
Vegetarian Eats

Our recommendations for your Moroccan menu:

Breakfast Load up on pastries, pancakes, fresh fruit and fresh squeezed juice. Fresh goat's cheese and olives from the souq are solid savoury choices with fresh baked *khoobz* (wood-fired pita bread).

Lunch Dive into *mezze* (salad selection) at restaurants, ranging from delicate cucumbers in orange-blossom water to substantial herbed beets laced with kaffir lime.

Dinner Look on menus for Berber tajine, which is vegetarian, or a vegetarian couscous. *Briouats* (cigar shaped pastries stuffed with goat's cheese or egg and herbs) make a great starter.

a pasta dish or burger. (☏ 0524 37 59 04; www.terrassedesepices.com; 15 Souq Cherifia; mains Dh95-130; ⏱ 11am-10pm; 🍴)

Dar Moha

MOROCCAN $$$

20 Map p44, C2

Mohamed Fedal is Morocco's foremost celebrity chef, giving tastebuds a treat with updated local classics. The evening *diffa* (feast) is a five-course extravaganza that highlights the Moroccan sweet-savoury obsession. Make the most of the evening by eating little beforehand and, in warmer months, reserve a table by the pool. (☏ 0524 38 64 00; www.

darmoha.ma; 81 Rue Dar el-Bacha; lunch mains Dh90-220, 5-course set menu dinner Dh530; ⏱ noon-4pm & 7.30-10pm)

Villa Flore

MEDITERRANEAN $$

21 Map p44, D3

Dine in this art deco black-and-white riad on couscous sweetened by cinnamon and quince or meltingly tender confit lamb, presented with flair by stylish waiters. The food can be a bit so-so, but the atmosphere – sitting with a glass of wine in a sunny courtyard right in the heart of the medina, – is tranquil bliss after a day among the souqs. (☏ 0524 39 17 00; www.villa-flore.com; 4 Derb Azzouz; mains Dh60-140; ⏱ 12.30-3pm & 7.30-11pm Wed-Mon)

Drinking

Dar Cherifa

CAFE

22 Map p44, D4

Ring the doorbell to be admitted into this serene late-15th-century Saadian riad. Tea, juice and saffron coffee are served on ultra-comfy yellow sofas in a courtyard framed by soaring blush-pink pillars topped with intricate cedar lintels. Surrounding salons are home to art exhibitions and you'll get great views from the terrace upstairs. (☏ 0524 42 64 63; 8 Derb Chorfa Lakbir; ⏱ noon-7pm; 🛜)

Café Arabe

BAR

23 Map p44, E3

Gloat over souq purchases with cocktails on the roof or alongside the

Tea time at Dar Cherifa

Zen *zellij* (ceramic tile mosaic) courtyard fountain. Prices here are reasonable for such a stylish place, and you can order half bottles of decent Moroccan wines such as the peppery red Siroua S. The food is bland but the company isn't – artists and designers flock here. (📞0524 42 97 28; www.cafearabe.com; 184 Rue Mouassine; ⏱10am-midnight; 🛜)

Terrasse des Teinturiers   CAFE

24 📍 Map p44, E3

Souqs exhausting you? Climb up the stairs here to find a little rooftop oasis high above the haggling din. There's cold juice and soothing mint tea, as well as tajines (Dh60) if you're hungry. (8 Souq Sebbaghine; ⏱11am-10pm)

Bazaar Cafe   CAFE

25 📍 Map p44, D4

Head straight up to the rooftop for sweeping views out to the Atlas Mountains, and relax with wine or beer and some tapas-style snacks. This intimate cafe-restaurant has a chilled ambience – just the ticket for taking a break after sightseeing. (📞0524 38 72 83; www.bazaarcafe.ma; 24 Rue Sidi el-Yamani; ⏱noon-11.30pm)

Café Atay   CAFE

26 📍 Map p44, E1

There's a striking Mediterranean-island vibe going on at this cute cafe's rooftop, which is all rattan shades and white-cane furniture, with only the subtlest

LONELY PLANET/GETTY IMAGES ©

Musicians performing at Dar Moha (p52)

Understand
Marrakesh's Fondouqs

Fondouqs (rooming houses; also known as caravanserais) once dotted the important stopover towns on Morocco's caravan routes. Since medieval times, these creative courtyard complexes provided ground-floor stables and workshops, and rented rooms for desert traders and travelling merchants upstairs – and from this flux of artisans and adventurers emerged the inventive culture of modern-day Marrakesh. As trading communities became more stable and affluent, however, most *fondouqs* were gradually replaced with private homes and storehouses.

Only 140 *fondouqs* remain in the medina, many of them now converted into artisan complexes, and although you'll find them in various states of disrepair, many retain fine original woodcarving, romantic balconies and even some stucco work. Poke your head in to admire the well-travelled, shop-worn glory of some of the best examples, found on Rue Dar el-Bacha and Rue Mouassine.

touches of the typical Marrakesh aesthetic on show. It's a very cool place to hang out, idle over a pot of tea, or fill up on a menu (Dh40 to Dh75) that wanders from tajines to ravioli. (☎0661 34 42 46; 62 Rue Amesfah; ⏱11am-10pm; 🛜)

Shopping

Souk Cherifa   DESIGN

27 🔒 Map p44, E2

Short-circuit souq fatigue and head straight for this converted *fondouq* where younger local designers congregate on the upper floor. Pick up funky cushion covers at **Sisi Morocco**, colourful kaftans and clutches made from carpets at **Khmissa**, contemporary embroidered linens from **La Maison Bahira** (www.maisonbahira.com), and top quality argan oil, *amlou* (argannut butter) and beauty products at **Arganino**. (Souq Kchachbia; ⏱10am-7pm)

Al Kawtar   ARTS & CRAFTS

28 🔒 Map p44, E2

This nonprofit female collective not only trains women with disabilities in embroidery craft but also sells fine homewares, with a sharp eye for converting traditional needlework into snazzily modern pieces. Pick up a beautiful tablecloth or some gorgeous bed linen here; you know your money's going to a good cause. (☎0524 38 56 95; www.alkawtar.org; 3 Derb Zaouia Laftihia, Rue Mouassine; ⏱9.30am-2pm & 3-6.30pm)

Assouss Cooperative d'Argane   BEAUTY, FOOD & DRINK

29 🔒 Map p44, D3

This is the Marrakesh retail outlet of a women's argan cooperative outside Essaouira. The all-women staff will ply you with free samples of *amlou* and proudly explain how their ultra-emollient cosmetic oil and gourmet dipping oils are made. You'll find it near Mouassine Fountain. (☎0524 38 01 25; 94 Rue Mouassine; ⏱9am-1pm & 3-7pm Sat-Thu, 9am-noon Fri)

Top Tip
Surviving Faux-Guide Hassle

Marrakesh has done a stellar job cracking down on the medina's faux guides, but you may still be approached by hustlers trying to earn commission from shops. The following are useful tactics to deal with them:

▶ Politely decline offers of help you don't want. Exchange a few good humoured remarks but don't shake hands or get involved in lengthy conversation.

▶ Give the impression that you know where you're going. Say you hired a guide on your first day and now you'd like to explore solo.

▶ Retreat to a cafe if you start losing your cool. Mint tea is soul soothing!

Cooperative Artisanale des Femmes de Marrakesh

ARTS & CRAFTS

30 Map p44, E3

A showcase for Marrakesh's women *mâalems* (expert artisans), the cooperative is eye-opening and a total bargain. Original, handcrafted designs include handbags made from water-bottle caps wrapped in wool, hand-knitted *kissa* (hammam gloves) and black-and-white kaftans edged with red silk embroidery. Ask cooperative director Souad Boudeiry about getting tunics and dresses tailor-made. (0524 37 83 08; 67 Souq Kchachbia; 10am-1pm & 3.30-7pm Sat-Thu)

L'Art du Bain Savonnerie Artisanale

COSMETICS

31 Map p44, E3

Do your skin a favour with biodegradable, pure plant-oil soaps made in Marrakesh with fragrant blends of local herbs, flowers and spices. (0668 44 59 42; Souq Lebbadine; 10am-7pm Mon-Sat)

Maison du Caftan

CLOTHING

32 Map p44, D3

High-class and high-quality kaftans are the name of the game here, with suitably large price tags. Next door are gorgeous traditional textiles (bedspreads, tablecloths etc) featuring delicate embroidery. Worthy of a look, even if it's just to browse the range of different designs. (0524 44 10 51; 65 Rue Sidi el-Yamani)

Max & Jan

FASHION & ACCESSORIES

33 Map p44, E2

Quirky jewellery sits alongside vintage kaftans, slouchy active-wear and re-imagined salwar pants inside this funky boutique that puts the wacky and inspired into Moroccan fashion. (0524 37 55 70; www.maxandjan.ma; 14 Rue Amesfah; 10am-7pm)

Norya Ayron

FASHION & ACCESSORIES

Located in Le Jardin (see 17 Map p44, E2), Norya Ayron's bijoux boutique counts Maggie Gyllenhaal and

---

Understand

Argan Oil

Rich in vitamin E, argan oil must be the finest cosmetic ever to pass through the business end of a goat.

Outside Essaouira and in the Anti Atlas, goats climb low argan trees to eat the fruit, digesting the soft, fuzzy outer layer and passing the pit. Traditionally it is women who then collect the dung, and extract, clean and crack the pit to remove the nut, which is then pressed to yield the orange-tinted oil. This is arduous handwork. Buying argan oil from a shop run by a collective is the best way to ensure that the women are fairly paid.

Argan nuts being hand-processed into oil

Sharon Stone among its fans thanks to her contemporary take on traditional kaftans and *abeyyas* (women's garments) in often fabulously loud silk prints. Velvety soft suede and leather bags, kitsch clutches and a select range of jewellery mean you can deck yourself out in complete boho-bling. (www.norya-ayron.com; Le Jardin, 32 Rue Sidi Abdelaziz; ⏱11.30am-5pm & 7-10pm Wed-Mon, 11.30am-4pm Tue)

Galerie Le Coeur Blanc ART

34 🏠 Map p44, E2

Local artist Khantour Hamid displays and sells his work in the charmingly decrepit Fondouq Sarsar. His vibrant oil-on-canvas abstract scenes are full of the colour and mayhem of the city. (📞0667 96 75 97; 194 Rue Mouassine; ⏱10am-6pm)

Explore

Central Souqs

The lanes that spool north from Djemaa el-Fna sum up this old caravan city's charm. Scents of cumin and grilled meat intermingle in alleyways where shafts of sunlight strike through palm-frond roofing and hawkers bid you hello in 10 languages. Throw away your map and go get lost in the helter-skelter for a while.

The Sights in a Day

 The best time to stroll around the central souqs is before 11am when traffic (both human and two wheeled) is at its lowest. Take a coffee break at **Café des Épices** (p71) then head to **Musée Boucharouite** (p69) to get the low-down on one of Morocco's lesser-known crafts.

Late afternoon, when most of the bigger tour groups have dispersed, is a good time to check out a couple of Marrakesh's key sights. Pay a visit to **Musée de Marrakech** (p62) to gawp at the splendour that the ruling class swaddled themselves in, then gaze in awe at the majesty of the **Ali ben Youssef Medersa** (p60). Afterwards stroll to **Maison de la Photographie** (p64), where you can see the city through the eyes of the first photographers who ventured here.

Many souq stalls stay open for a few hours after dark, so it's a good time to shop if you don't like crowds. Otherwise, head out for a roof-top dinner and drink as the sun sets: this is chill-out time after a day within the medina hubbub.

For a local's day in the heart of the souqs, see p66.

Top Sights

Ali ben Youssef Medersa (p60)

Musée de Marrakech (p62)

Maison de la Photographie (p64)

Local Life

Discovering the Heart of the Souqs (p66)

Best of Marrakesh

Food
Naima (p71)

Shopping
Anamil (p74)

Maison de la Photographie (p64)

Dar Chrifa Lamrania (p74)

Chabi Chic (p74)

Berber Culture
Musée Boucharouite (p69)

Getting There

✈ **Walk** The most straightforward route from Djemaa el-Fna is to take Souq Semmarine (off Souq Quessabine) up to Place Rahba Kedima. From Mouassine, rather than losing yourself in the souqs, take the longer but simpler route via Rue Mouassine and Rue Amesfah.

Top Sights
Ali ben Youssef Medersa

Although founded in the 14th century under the Merenids, it was the Saadians – never a dynasty to turn down a grand building project – who bequeathed this *medersa* (theological college) with its dazzling decoration. Once the largest Quranic learning centre in North Africa, it remains today among the region's most splendid examples of Islamic art.

Map p68, B2

0524 44 18 93

Pl ben Youssef

admission Dh20

9am-7pm, to 6pm winter

Grand Entrance

'You who enter my door, may your highest hopes be exceeded.' So reads the inscription over the entrance to the Ali ben Youssef Medersa, and after six centuries, the blessing still works its charms on visitors. Carved cedar cupolas and *mashra biyya* (wooden-lattice screen) balconies lead the way in offering a taste of the artisanship within.

Courtyard Opulence

The *medersa* is a mind-boggling profusion of Hispano-Morish ornamentation. The courtyard, bordered by arcades on its north and south sides, is a cornucopia of five-colour *zellij* (ceramic tile mosaic) walls, stucco archways and cedar lintels with weather-worn carved vines. This would have been the main space where students at the *medersa* spent most of their day learning.

Stark Dormitories

While the students' learning space may have been sumptuously inspiring, their living quarters certainly weren't. Climb the stairs to the dormitory quarter and its series of poky rooms with views down into the courtyard below. Now imagine the fact that 900 students once lived here while they were studying religious and legal texts at the *medersa*.

The Beauty of the Mihrab

At the far end of the courtyard is the hall containing the mihrab (niche in a mosque indicating the direction of Mecca) made from prized, milky-white Italian Carrara marble. The decoration on the surrounding walls is remarkably well preserved, utilising typical palm and pine-cone motifs throughout.

☑ Top Tips

▶ For the best photography and views of the entire interior compound, head upstairs to the dormitories, where small windows allow great panoramas over the courtyard.

▶ Try to time your visit for late afternoon when the light is at its best and the large tour groups have mostly dispersed for the day.

✗ Take a Break

Chill out with a tea or chow down on a lunchtime tajine on the shady rooftop terrace of Kafe Merstan (p73).

If all this sightseeing has worked up a healthy appetite, make a beeline to Naima (p71) for some serious couscous action.

Top Sights
Musée de Marrakech

If the Mnebhi Palace walls could talk they sure could tell some tales. Once home to Mehdi Mnebhi, defence minister during Sultan Moulay Abdelaziz's reign (1894–1908), these sumptuous salons were later filched by Pasha Glaoui. After independence the palace became a school, but a 1997 restoration swung open its doors to the masses as a museum.

👁 Map p68, B2

📞 0524 44 18 93

www.museedemarra
kech.ma

Pl ben Youssef

adult/child Dh50/free

🕐 9am-7pm, to 6pm
Oct-Mar

Palatial Kitchens

The most sedate interiors inside the palace are found in the old kitchens area, where the green tile floors and white plaster walls hold only touches of *zellij* decoration. Now home to the Moroccan Contemporary Art Exhibition, the walls are hung with works by renowned local artists such as Abderrahim Yamou, Mohamed Nabili and Kamal Lahbabi.

Inner Courtyard

Mnebhi Palace's inner courtyard (enclosed by a roof) is a riot of cedar-wood archways, stained-glass windows, intricate painted door panels and, of course, lashings of *zellij* tilework. It's all overlooked by a whopper of a brass lamp that hangs above the central fountain. The surrounding salons have exhibits on Moroccan textiles, tea traditions and ceramics.

Dazzling Ceramics

The main room off the inner courtyard is home to a fine collection of highly decorative Fez ceramics demonstrating the elaborate blue-and-white geometric designs that made this style of work so prized. Most of the pieces date from the 19th century when Fez's artisans were still mixing local minerals to create the distinct blue shade for which their pottery became recognised.

Palace Hammam

The three domed rooms here are a typical example of traditional hammam architecture. Enter through a narrow corridor to reach the *frigidariam* (cold room), the *tepidarium* (warm room) and then the *caldarium* (hot room). All the rooms are minimally decorated with only the domed ceilings hosting colourful geometric designs and daubs of simple ochre-red patterns bordering doorways.

☑ **Top Tips**

▶ The glitzy inner courtyard of the palace is a photographer's dream, but because the roof has been closed over you may need to know how to use your camera's white balance settings to achieve photos without a yellowish cast.

▶ The museum's Moroccan artworks may not be particularly well laid out or labelled, but the real reason for a visit is the palace's interior decoration.

✗ **Take a Break**

You don't need to step far from the museum to take a break. The entrance courtyard has a charming cafe with plenty of shady seating where you can rest up and enjoy a mint tea.

For something more local, stroll across Place ben Youssef to tuck into meaty grills at Chez Abdelhay (p72).

Top Sights
Maison de la Photographie

When Parisian Patrick Menac'h and Marrakshi Hamid Mergani realised they were both collecting vintage Moroccan photography, they decided to open a gallery to show their collections in their original context, and so Maison de la Photographie was born. The result is a fascinating display of the lifestyles and landscapes that the first intrepid photographers in Morocco captured through their lenses.

◉ Map p68, D2

☎ 0524 38 57 21

www.maisondelaphotographie.ma

46 Souq el-Fassi

adult/child Dh40/free

🕓 9.30am-7pm

Vintage Portraiture

Most of the ground floor is devoted to portraiture, with a mesmerising photo of Hamidou Laambre, taken by Arevalo in 1885, being the stand-out picture of the collection. The small room leading towards the staircase contains photographs of Marrakesh in the 1920s. In particular, check out the 1926 photo of the Saadian Tombs after they'd just been rediscovered.

Morocco's Photography Debut

The ground floor's back salon holds the gallery's oldest photos, showing the debut of photography in Morocco when the first Europeans arrived with cameras and began documenting life here. The exhibit includes images of Tangier taken between 1870 and 1900, as well as a collection of postcards that were reproduced from the work of these early photographers.

Landscapes & Lifestyles

On the 1st floor, the chambers surrounding the balcony host pictures displaying the lifestyles and landscapes of Morocco in the early 20th century. Don't miss the thoroughly engaging images taken by Hungarian photographer Nicolas Muller in the 1940s, or the 1920 photo of Marrakesh's ramparts, with only empty desert stretching to the horizon outside the walls.

High Atlas Life

As you climb the stairs to the rooftop terrace, pop into the small room where Daniel Chicault's intimate photographs of High Atlas life are displayed and his High Atlas documentary is played. Filmed in 1956, the documentary is a fascinating view into rural life during that period and was the first colour documentary made in Morocco.

☑ Top Tips

▶ Useful information cards (in several languages) are kept in wall folders throughout the gallery, aiding understanding of the images and the history of photography in Morocco.

▶ A small shop at the entry sells editioned prints from the original negatives of many of the works displayed in the gallery – a great souvenir idea.

✗ Take a Break

You have ample reason to linger after you've finished viewing the exhibits. The Maison de la Photographie's panoramic rooftop terrace is perfect for a coffee or mint tea.

Otherwise, step next door to Dar Tazi (p72) to feast on a three-course set menu.

Local Life
Discovering the Heart of the Souqs

The very core of Marrakesh is a medley of buying, selling, haggling and hawking, but it's not all about carpets, pashminas and twinkly lamps – although, you'll find those as well. Here you'll see metalworkers busy at their trade, apothecaries with tiny shops full of exotic herbal remedies and Marrakshis doing their shopping at hole-in-the-wall butcher's shops and vegetable carts.

....

1 Spice Action at Place Rahba Kedima

Begin your stroll in Place Rahba Kedima, rimmed by spice shops. You'll notice some rather unusual products if you look closely. Moroccans utilise their local spice stall as a one-stop shop for natural remedies to cure sickness and ailments, and potions to eliminate mischievous *djin* (spirits), as well as for items to pep up their cooking.

❷ The Carpet Souq

With its cheerful shopkeepers and the rainbow hued rugs that swing from every hook, it's hard to believe that **Creiee Berbere** was ever the scene of anything more harmful than the odd wily carpet dealer tout. But this enclosed square once functioned as Marrakesh's main slave market, where the human cargo of the caravan trade were bought and sold.

❸ Into the Qissariat

The zigzagging alleys that lie between Souq el-Kebir and Souq Smata are the *qissariat*. Although a smattering of tourist-oriented shops have moved in, this is very much a local haunt with rows of teensy *jellaba* and *babouches* (leather slippers) stalls. If you get a bit lost, don't worry. You'll always end up back on one of the main souq streets.

❹ Blacksmiths at Work

One of the most interesting souqs to wander is **Souq Haddadine** (Blacksmith's Souq), full of busy workshops where the sound of the metalworkers' hammers provides a staccato background beat. If you've been tempted by some of those lovely Moroccan lamps for sale throughout the souqs, buying direct here will probably get you the best price.

❺ A Local Lunch

Feeling adventurous? Just behind Souq Haddadine's tangle of lanes the blacksmith clanging subsides to be replaced by the sizzle of grilled meat.

The **Ben Youssef Food Stalls** (off Souq Chaaria; mains Dh25-40; ⏰11.30am-3.30pm) serve up meat skewers, and the occasional stewed sheep's head, to a lunchtime crew of hungry souq workers. Pull up a pew and eat whatever looks fresh.

❻ Leather-Hide Workshops

Take a stroll in the **leatherworker's alley** nearby where the stalls are piled high with leather hides ready to be turned into all those handbags you see swinging throughout the main souqs. Often (mostly during morning hours) you can see freshly dyed leather hides left out to dry in the sun in Place Ben Youssef.

❼ Central Vegetable Market

This local vegetable market is where Marrakshis living in the central medina area come wielding their baskets to stock up on fruit, herbs and fresh local produce that's laid out for show at stalls and upon blankets on the cobblestones. For a snack, pick up some fruit here; haggling isn't necessary.

❽ Through the Butcher's Alley

Locals don't need to walk far to tick off the rest of their shopping list; the lane leading south from the vegetable market is lined with small butcher's stores. Check out the entrails and offal on display, and the carcasses swinging from hooks, as you walk through on the way back to Place Rahba Kedima.

A   **B**   **C**   **D**

0 ━━━━━━━━ 100 m
0 ━━━━━━━━ 0.05 miles

R Riad Laârous

R Amesfah

R Souq el-Fassi

17

Dar Bellarj

2

Ali ben Youssef Mosque 5

Ali ben Youssef Medersa

13

15 11

Maison de la Photographie

19

R Mouassine

10

3 Koubba Ba'adiyn

Souq Chaaria

Musée de Marrakech

Souq Kchachbia

KÂAT BEN NAHID

Souq Smata

22

14

Souq Nejarine

Souq el-Kebir (Souq Nejarine)

Souq Chkaira

Derb Sidi Ishak

20

7

Rue Azbezt

Bradia El Kedima

Souq Lebbadine

CENTRAL SOUQS

6

Ben Salah Mosque

Derb Sidi Ishak

1

Musée Boucharouite

Taoulat Ben Saleh

Souq Stailia

8

Rahba Kedima

18

Place Rahba Kedima

4

16

12

21

MOUASSINE

9

Zinkat Rahba

R Laksour

Souq Semmarine

R Blyapine

Derb Moulay Abdelkader

Place Bab Fteuh

Souq Quessabine

Kenaria Dabachi

Derb Debachi

R des Banques

For reviews see

◉ Top Sights   p60
◉ Sights   p69
✕ Eating   p71
🍷 Drinking   p73
🛍 Shopping   p74

Ali ben Youssef Medersa complex (p60)

Sights

Musée Boucharouite   MUSEUM

1 ◉ Map p68, C3

Berber *boucharouites* (rag rugs made from recycled cloth) may be a poor cousin to the famous jewel-toned Moroccan carpets, but this beautifully collated gallery housed in an 18th-century riad displays the artistry of the lesser-known craft. The museum is the work of avid collector Patrick de Maillard, and in addition to *boucharouites* the rooms are scattered with a lovely jumble of Moroccan popular art, from agricultural implements to painted doors. The terrace upstairs serves refreshments. (📞0524 38 38 87; Derb El Cadi; adult/child Dh40/free; ⊙9.30am-6pm Mon-Sat, closed Aug)

Dar Bellarj   GALLERY

2 ◉ Map p68, B1

Flights of fancy come with the territory at Dar Bellarj, a stork hospital (*bellarj* is Arabic for stork) turned into Marrakesh's premier arts centre. Each year the nonprofit Dar Bellarj Foundation adopts a program theme, ranging from film to women's textiles and storytelling. Calligraphy demonstrations, art openings, craft exhibits and arts workshops are regular draws, and admission is usually free (there's a charge for some events). (📞0524 44 45 55; www.darbellarj.org; 9-7 Toualate Zaouiate

Top Tip
Navigating the Souqs

Got your map ready? Well, it's probably of little use to you here. There are a couple of tricks, though, that will help you unravel the souq spaghetti-sprawl:

▶ Don't forget to look up: many souqs have street names placed at the top of their arched entrances.

▶ Don't automatically trust those 'To Djemaa el-Fna' signs hanging from souq ceilings; some of them take you on ridiculously roundabout routes.

▶ If you need to ask directions, ask a shopkeeper; mischievous children (and some bored young men) deliberately mislead tourists.

Lahdar; admission free; ⏱9.30am-12.30pm & 2-5.30pm Mon-Sat)

Koubba Ba'adiyn   HISTORIC BUILDING

 3 Map p68, B2

The Almohads destroyed almost everything their Almoravid predecessors built in Marrakesh, but overlooked this small, graceful 12th-century *koubba* (shrine) – probably used for ablutions – across from Ali ben Youssef Mosque. This relic reveals what Hispano-Morish architecture owes to the Almoravids: keyhole arches, ribbed vaulting, interlaced arabesques and domed cupolas on crenellated bases. It's closed to visitors but you can peek through the fence to get a glimpse of its architectural details. (Pl ben Youssef)

Rahba Kedima   SQUARE

 4 Map p68, B4

Harry and the Hogwarts crowd probably shop here for school supplies. The Rahba Kedima plaza is ringed with apothecaries who sell exotic and mysterious spell supplies to locals, and spice mixtures and traditional cosmetics to tourists. The middle of the square is home to stalls selling Berber hats and woven baskets. (Pl Rahba Kedima)

Ali ben Youssef Mosque   MOSQUE

5 Map p68, B2

This mosque is affiliated with the nearby Ali ben Youssef Medersa (p60), and its minaret is the major landmark looming over Place ben Youssef. The first mosque built here by the Almoravids was subsequently demolished by their Almohad successors who, in turn, built their own mosque in its place. (Place ben Youssef; ⏱closed to non-Muslims)

Ben Salah Mosque   MOSQUE

 6 Map p68, D3

The minaret of this Merinid-era mosque (dating from 1321) still holds on to its green ceramic-tile detailing. (Derb Sidi Ishak)

Eating

Naima   MOROCCAN **$$**

7 Map p68, C3

If you want to eat couscous prepared by a proper Marrakshi mamma then Naima is it. Squeeze into the tiny dining room, order either tajine or couscous (there's no menu) and settle back with a mint tea as the women get cooking. Bring your appetite: this is family-style Moroccan food and the portions are huge.
(Derb Sidi Ishak; meals Dh100; ☺11am-10pm)

Café des Épices   CAFE **$**

8 Map p68, B4

A traveller's institution parked in prime position on Rahba Kedima.

Watch the henna ladies and basket sellers tout for business from your shady stool while munching on sandwiches or sipping freshly squeezed beetroot, apple and ginger juice. We like the Paris Marrakech burger stuffed with cheese and aubergine. (☎0254 39 17 70; Pl Rahba Kedima; sandwich & salads Dh45-60; ☺8am-9pm; 🛜)

Nomad   MEDITERRANEAN **$$**

9 Map p68, B4

Nomad's rooftop terrace is one of the medina's buzziest eating venues. The small menu adds contemporary tweaks to North African staples such as a spice-packed Tunisian lamb *briq* (pie), while keeping the punters happy by also serving up a flavoursome

---

Understand
Understanding Islam

Soaring minarets, shimmering mosaics, intricate calligraphy, the muezzin's call to prayer: much of what thrills visitors in Marrakesh today is inspired by a deep faith in Islam. Islam is built on five pillars: *shahada*, the affirmation of faith in God and God's word entrusted to the Prophet Mohammed; *salat* (prayer), ideally performed five times daily; *zakat* (charity), a moral obligation to give to those in need; *sawn*, the daytime fasting practised during the month of Ramadan; and *haj*, the pilgrimage to Mecca that is the culmination of lifelong faith for Muslims.

One of the biggest disappointments for non-Muslim visitors to Marrakesh who are interested in Islamic history is that they are not allowed to enter Muslim religious buildings. This decree dates back to the French protectorate era when French resident-général Lyautey banned non-Muslims from entering mosques to avoid conflict. Luckily everyone can contemplate the artistry of Islamic design within the Ali ben Youssef Medersa (p60) and also see the skilled artisan work on the Koutoubia's *minbar* (prayer pulpit) that now sits in Badi Palace (p89).

Local Life

I Limoni

We're kinda partial to any restaurant that has a collection of kitsch snow globes on display, but **I Limoni** (Map p68, B2; 📞 0524 38 30 30; 40 Rue Bab Taghzout; mains Dh80-180; 🕙noon-11pm; 🌿) serves up a fine line of pasta as well. Park yourself up in the lemon-tree-shaded courtyard; order a glass of wine (from Dh50); and tuck into comforting dishes such as ricotta ravioli with parmesan, lemon zest and mint.

Turn left just after the **Chrob ou Chouf fountain** (Rue Assouel) to find it.

burger. Desserts such as apple and beetroot clafoutis and hibiscus panna cotta add an interesting end-of-dinner twist. (📞0524 38 16 09; www.nomadmarrakech.com; 1 Derb Arjan; mains Dh90-120; 🕙11am-11pm; 🌐🌿)

Chez Abdelhay

MOROCCAN $

 10 Map p68, A2

Firing up the grill from their cubby-hole kitchen, these guys dish up hearty, simple meals of grilled meat that come with sides of salad, Berber-style omelette and some seriously delicious lentils for a tasty, filling lunch. Tables are spread across the alleyway outside. Find it by heading up the northwest lane that leads off Place ben Youssef. (off Pl Ben Youssef; meals Dh50; 🕙11am-3.30pm)

Dar Tazi

MOROCCAN $$

 11 Map p68, D2

We like the smiley staff and the efficient service here. The restaurant itself has plenty of old-fashioned, homy appeal and the three-course set menu, featuring fresh salads, *kefta* (meatballs) and plenty of lamb-and-prune tajine goodness, will leave you set for the night. (📞0524 37 83 82; Rue Souq el-Fazzi; set menu Dh120; 🕙11.30am-10pm)

Dar TimTam

MOROCCAN $$

 12 Map p68, B4

The bow-tied waiters and old-fashioned table linen may seem a bit fusty, but the courtyard of this 18th-century riad is a tranquil spot for a light lunch. Steer clear of the à la carte menu with its overpriced dishes and instead order a rejuvenating mint tea and a generous assortment of eight Moroccan salads (Dh95). (📞0524 39 14 46; Zinkat Rahba; meals Dh95-250; 🕙11.30am-4pm; 🌿)

Le Foundouk

INTERNATIONAL $$$

 13 Map p68, C2

A spidery iron chandelier lit with candles sets the mood for fine dining, with a choice of Moroccan and European menus. When the food lives up to the decor, it's fabulous, and when not, well, at least you got your money's worth for atmosphere. It's a great choice just for drinks at the bar as well. (📞0524 37 81 90; www.foundouk.com; 55 Souq el-Fassi; mains Dh100-200; 🕙7pm-midnight Tue-Sun; 🌐)

Drinking

Kafe Merstan
CAFE

 Map p68, C3

Escape the hustle and bustle to hang out on Merstan's roof terrace with a fresh juice, or mint or cinnamon tea. Friendly service, comfy shaded seating and good views make this a popular spot to refresh and recharge right in the centre of the medina souqs. (☎0524 38 67 65; 2 Souq Chaaria; ☺10am-10pm)

Maison de la Photographie Terrace
CAFE

 Map p68, D2

This panoramic terrace is a wonderful place to sit back and admire the view with a fruit juice or mint tea after visiting the photography gallery (p64) downstairs. (☎0524 38 57 21; www.maison-delaphotographie.com; 46 Souq el-Fassi; ☺9.30am-7pm)

Chez Maazouz
CAFE

 Map p68, B4

An easygoing place with decent coffee, great tea and fresh juices that is perfectly placed to catch the shopping-weary as they stumble out of the souqs. Head up the rickety stairs for views over Place Rahba Kedima or throw yourself down in the shady seating out the front. (☎0661 51 42 11; 192 Pl Rahba Kedima; ☺10.30am-9pm)

Saffron being weighed

DANA MCLIMAHAN/GETTY IMAGES©

Understand
Saffron

Saffron – the gold dust of the foodie world – is for sale throughout Marrakesh's souqs. But hold on to your cooking aprons, gourmet travellers. Not all of it is exactly what it seems. That really cheap saffron that spice stalls are hawking for Dh10 to Dh20 per gram? That's usually safflower. Real saffron (the stigmas of the saffron crocus) have a more delicate thread, are less garishly red than safflower and have a tiny yellow tip. It costs about Dh60 per gram.

Shopping

Dar Chrifa Lamrania
ART

17 🔒 Map p68, B1

There are plenty of little art studios dotted around the medina, but this particular one displays some of the more interesting and original paintings by local artists. To find it, head past the Medersa Ali ben Youssef and turn left. It's tucked under the next arch. (📞0663 47 33 23; 11 Zaouit Lahdar; ⊙10.30am-7pm)

Fondouq Namas
CARPETS

18 🔒 Map p68, B4

Several carpet dealers have their shops here, with piles and piles of beautiful Berber *kilims* and *hanbels* (pileless woven carpets) in a range of prices. There are plenty of Berber blankets and other tribal trappings for those looking to take home something smaller as well. Get your glass of mint tea in hand and start carpet-hunting. (Derb Sidi Ishak; ⊙10am-7.30pm)

Bennouna Faissal Weaving
TEXTILES

19 🔒 Map p68, D2

This friendly workshop and store sells fixed-price hand-loomed cotton, wool, silk and linen textiles of exceptional quality. You're welcome to watch them work the looms as you have a relaxed browse for bed linen and scarves. Prices are higher than elsewhere, but some of their products are truly beautiful and unique. (25 Souq el-Fassi; ⊙10am-5pm)

Anamil
ARTS & CRAFTS

20 🔒 Map p68, C3

Step inside this little treasure trove and you're bound to fall in love with at least one beautiful thing. The extremely well collated collection of high-quality ceramics, textiles, soft leather handbags and lamps is full of gorgeous gifts that are a little bit different, and a tad more quirky, than you'll see elsewhere in the souqs. (48 Derb Sidi Ishak; ⊙9.30am-6pm)

Chabi Chic
HOMEWARES

This foodie-traveller haven located under Nomad Restaurant (see 9 ✖ Map p68, B4) is dedicated to Moroccan kitchenware. Pick up beautifully packaged orange-flower water and spice-blend mixes to pep up your kitchen displays back home. The thoroughly modern stripy tajine bowls

☑ Top Tip

Shop Till You Drop

Planning to hit the souqs for some shopping when you get into town?

▸ Pack a reusable shopping bag. Morocco banned plastic bags in 2016. Help souq stall vendors stick to the rules by toting your own.

▸ Wear decent walking shoes – you'll be grateful after a long day trudging through the souqs.

Understand
Marrakesh Haggling Guide
– – – – – – – – – – – – – – – –

Haggling can be great fun as long as you go into it with the right attitude. The most important note to remember is that both you and the seller are trying to reach a satisfactory agreement. The vendor is not going to sell an object for a loss; if you can't reach a mutually beneficial price, you simply walk away.

Dos & Don'ts
▶ Don't try out your bargaining skills when you're tired and grumpy. You're not likely to make a great deal and it will be a thoroughly unenjoyable experience.

▶ Do exchange pleasantries first with the shopkeeper. Don't even think about kicking off negotiations without saying hello and asking how they are.

▶ Do work out what you'd be willing to pay for something you like, before you ask the price.

▶ Do always accept the mint tea if it's offered.

The Haggling Process
The initial price the vendor quotes may have nothing to do with the item's actual value, so don't rely on that figure for your counter offer. Depending on the vendor (and their perception of how much money you may have) their first quote may be exceedingly high or not far off the value of the item. This is why it's important that you've already worked out what your maximum offering will be.

Counter with an offer that's about one-third of your maximum limit and let the negotiations begin. Keep it friendly. Bargaining should never get nasty. If you're starting to feel pressured or you get a bad vibe from the seller, walk away.

Walking away when you can't reach an agreement is fine. Offering a price you're not willing to pay and then walking away is considered the height of bad manners. Make sure you actually want the item before starting to haggle.

Berber carpets for sale

Understand
Carpet Buying For Beginners

This quick guide to Morocco's carpets will help you on your hunt for the perfect rug in the souqs.

Rabati Plush pile carpets in deep jewel tones, featuring an ornate central motif balanced by fine border details. Rabati carpets are highly prized, and could run to Dh2000 per sq metre.

Chichaoua Simple and striking, with zigzags, asterisks and enigmatic symbols on a variegated red or purple background (about Dh700 to Dh1000 per sq metre).

Hanbels or kilims These are flat weaves with no pile. Some *hanbels* include Berber letters and auspicious symbols such as the evil eye, Southern Cross and Berber *fibule* (brooch) in their weave (about Dh700 to Dh900 per sq metre).

Zanafi or glaoua *Kilims* and shag carpeting, together at last. Opposites attract in these rugs, where sections of fluffy pile alternate with flat-woven stripes or borders. These are usually Dh1000 to Dh1750 per sq metre.

Shedwi Flat weaves with bold patterns in black wool on off-white. For as little as Dh400 for a smaller rug, they're impressive yet inexpensive gifts.

and Moroccan tea-glass sets could put the 'wow' in your next dinner party. (📞0524 38 15 46; www.chabi-chic.com; 1 Derb Arjan, under Nomad Restaurant; 🕙9.30am-6pm)

Apothicaire Tuareg FOOD
21 🛍 Map p68, B4

Serious foodies, you have found spice nirvana. Proprietor Abdel is happy to take shoppers through a spice 101. His old-fashioned shop is crammed to the rafters with both day-to-day cooking spices and the more bizarre natural remedies that Moroccans use to cure illnesses and scare away mischievous *djin* (spirits). (186 Pl Rahba Kedima; 🕙9am-7pm)

Herboristerie Talâa FOOD
22 🛍 Map p68, B2

The friendly English-speaking staff here can sort out all your spice needs. If you want to smother yourself in the scents of the souq, they have a vast selection of natural jasmine and amber perfumes and moisturising creams. (13 Souq Talâa; 🕙9.30am-6pm)

Local Life
Exploring Around Bab Debbagh

Getting There

🚶 **Walk** From the central souks, go along Souq el-Fassi, cross Rue Issebtiyne, and continue on Rue de Bab Debbagh to the medina gate.

🚕 **Taxi** No more than Dh10 from Bab Doukkala or Djemaa el-Fna.

This corner of the medina is where the workaday face of the old city comes to life. Here, the stench of the tanneries, buzzing bric-a-brac market and pilgrims paying their respects at local *marabout* (saint) shrines reveal a city deeply steeped in the traditions of old. Branch out from the souqs' core to explore this lesser-seen side of Marrakesh.

❶ At the City Gate
Bab Debbagh was built by the Almoravids as part of the city's fortifications and is Marrakesh's most interesting surviving gate. Notice how the narrow entry passageway forms a zigzag route. This simple architectural mechanism allowed Marrakesh's troops to have the upper hand if any invading force tried to breach the city.

❷ Into the Tanneries
You've found Marrakesh's **tanneries** (Rue de Bab Debbagh; ☺Sat-Thu) when you notice that acrid smell. Tanners work through the mornings transforming leather hides into a rainbow of hues. It's hard, dirty work and dangerous too, now that natural dyes have been eschewed for chemical colours.

❸ Walking down Rue Assouel
Busy Rue Assouel is miles away from the tourist-oriented souqs. No one is trying to sell you a carpet here. They're too busy doing their vegetable shopping or grabbing a quick snack from a local grill-stand while the sound of the blacksmith workshops echo over the road.

❹ Bab Kechich Market
Full of wacky bric-a-brac, this market just outside the ramparts at Bab Kechich is a local scene where vendors display everything from art deco ornaments to motorbike spare parts. You never know what little gem you could unearth while sifting through the motley jumble. Stroll around the stalls until you come to Bab el-Khemis.

❺ Zawiya Sidi Bel-Abbes
Moroccans believe that just being in the vicinity of a *marabout* confers *baraka* (a state of grace) and the **Zawiya Sidi Bel-Abbes** (Rue Sidi Ghalom) is Marrakesh's most important *marabout* shrine. Non-Muslims cannot enter the shrine itself, but can walk through the arched arcade, with its imposing gate, and into the courtyard to admire the elaborately decorated *zawiya* entranceway.

❻ Along Rue Bab Taghzout
The bijou candy-striped gate of Bab Taghzout heralds your entry onto Rue Bab Taghzout, which is lined with workshops, tiny clothing stores displaying the latest female jellaba fashions and *passementerie* (trims) shops.

❼ Medina Lifestyles Museum
Once home to Marrakshi poet Ben Omar, the **Musée de l'Art de Vivre** (Derb Chérif; adult/child Dh40/free; ☺9am-6pm) holds a small but well-collated collection of antique kaftans and *babouches* (leather slippers) from the 19th century. There's a shady courtyard cafe where you can relax with a pot of tea.

❽ At the 'Drink & Look'
Finish your stroll at the **Chrob ou Chouf** (Rue Assouel). The 'Drink and Look' fountain retains shreds of former finery with its intricately carved cedar-wood lintel. Unlike other fountains, this is still used and you'll likely see passing pedestrians stopping for a quick drink as you admire the artistry.

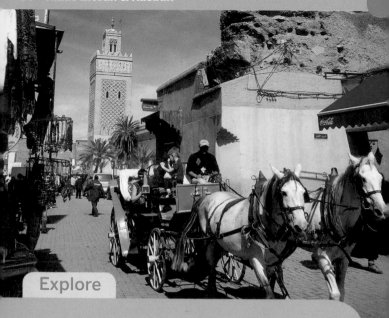

Explore

Riads Zitoun & Kasbah

Minimalism and Marrakesh high society definitely don't mix. With a mausoleum that's almost worth dying for and sumptuous palaces of long-gone pashas and sultans, this neighbourhood puts the bling in the medina. When your neck aches from all the ceiling-gazing, seek out the *mellah*: the alleys of this old Jewish quarter are a contemplative contrast to all that razzle-dazzle.

The Sights in a Day

☀️ Check out the salons of **Dar Si Said** (p86) and the exhibits of **Maison Tiskiwin** (p89) in the morning, before soaking up the quiet atmosphere of the *mellah* (Jewish quarter) in all its labyrinthine laneway charm. For a peaceful interlude, stroll through the **Miaâra Jewish Cemetery** (p90). Afterwards, put your feet up at bustling Place des Ferblantiers for lunch.

☀️ Spend the afternoon in monument-hopping mode. First head to **Bahia Palace** (p82) for Moroccan interior overload, then say hello to the rampart storks on a stroll through once-triumphant **Badi Palace** (p89). As the afternoon light turns golden, make a beeline for the **Saadian Tombs** (p84) to see the glory of this mausoleum.

🌙 For sunset views with dinner, nab a rooftop table at **Dar Anika** (p91) or, to end the day with a slice of culture, stroll on to funky **Cafe Clock** (p91), which hosts a program of evening events ranging from live music to storytelling. If you fancy a nightcap to top off the day, swerve on back to Place des Ferblantiers for a cold beer at **Kosybar** (p95).

👁 **Top Sights**

Bahia Palace (p82)

Saadian Tombs (p84)

Dar Si Said (p86)

💗 **Best of Marrakesh**

Food

PepeNero (p92)

Dar Anika (p91)

Berber Culture

Maison Tiskiwin (p89)

Cafe Clock (p91)

Dar Si Said (p86)

Bars & Nightlife

Kosybar (p95)

Getting There

🚶 **Walk** It's a 15-minute walk from Djemaa el-Fna; head straight down Rue Riad Zitoun el-Jedid or Rue Riad Zitoun el-Kedim.

🚗 **Taxi** Ask for Palais de la Bahia or Place des Ferblantiers. Taxis drop you next to the square (across the road from the palace).

Calèche The scenic option. Hire a horse-drawn carriage from their stand off Djemaa el-Fna.

Top Sights
Bahia Palace

Imagine the pomp and splendour you'd dream up with Morocco's top artisans at your beck and call, and here you have it. La Bahia (the Beautiful) is a floor-to-ceiling extravagance of intricate marquetry and *zouak* (painted wood) ceilings, begun by Grand Vizier Si Moussa in the 1860s but embellished from 1894 to 1900 by slave-turned-vizier Abu 'Bou' Ahmed.

👁 Map p88, C2

☎ 0524 38 95 64

Rue Riad Zitoun el-Jedid

adult/child Dh10/3

🕙 9am-4.30pm

Le Petit Riad

Let your eyes adjust to the dim light in the main salon, where the palace's intricate ornamentation comes into full view. Excepting the statement fireplace, the room is starkly devoid of furnishings, making the artisan work upon the ceilings and walls even more striking. Then step through an arcade of exquisitely carved arches into the verdant courtyard (La Petite Cour).

La Grande Cour

The Grand Courtyard (La Grande Cour) is an immense expanse of Italian Carrara marble rimmed by a gallery trimmed in jaunty blue and yellow. While admiring the tranquil effect of all that marble majesty, remember this is where people waited in the sun for hours to beg for Bou Ahmed's mercy. At the far end, backed by swaying palm trees, is the Room of Honour, featuring a spectacular cedar ceiling.

Le Grand Riad

Step through the doorway from the Grand Courtyard into the large courtyard of the Grand Riad, studded with fountains and lush foliage and sound-tracked by birdsong. This is the oldest part of the palace complex, completed in 1867. The salon here may be small, but it's bedecked with painted-wood artistry and stained-glass detailing.

The Harem

If you're going to envy a ceiling once in your life, it will be here. Running off the Grand Riad is the harem, which once housed Bou Ahmed's four wives and 24 concubines. The quarters of his favourite of the harem, Lalla Zineb, are the most spectacular, with original woven-silk panels, intricate marquetry and *zouak* ceilings of dazzling and colourful patterns painted with rose bouquets. Crane your neck upwards to spot the different floral motifs.

☑ Top Tips

▶ Tour groups tend to descend between 9.30am and 12.30pm. Try to come in the afternoon to beat the crowds.

▶ Even if you avoid peak time, you may encounter large tour groups. Patience is a virtue here. Come with plenty of time so you are able to admire the architecture and artisan work once they've passed by.

▶ The palm-shaded entry garden is a great place to stop for a minute and get your map bearings before heading back onto the street.

✕ Take a Break

If it's lunchtime, head to Dar Anika (p91) for rooftop dining on superb Moroccan dishes.

For an afternoon drink with a view, skip across the road to Kosybar (p95) in Place des Ferblantiers.

Top Sights
Saadian Tombs

Anyone who says you can't take it with you hasn't seen the Saadian Tombs. Sultan al-Mansour spared no expense on the Chamber of the 12 Pillars, making sure it would prolong his legend long after his death in 1603. He wasn't counting on Alawite sultan Moulay Ismail walling up the tombs a few decades later. The lavish mausoleum was only rediscovered in 1917.

👁 Map p88, A3

Rue de la Kasbah

adult/child Dh10/3

🕘9am-4.45pm

The Chamber of 12 Pillars

Imported Italian Carrara marble and gilded honeycomb *muqarnas* (decorative plasterwork) abound in the main chamber. All this glitz and gold surrounds the tombs of various Saadian princes and favoured members of the royal court. In particular, check out the hall's intricately carved *mihrab* (niche indicating the direction of Mecca), supported by a series of columns.

Al-Mansour's Final Resting Place

An opening at the hall's far end allows you a view of the central chamber, which holds the tomb of the man himself. Sultan Ahmed al-Mansour ed Dahbi's tomb lies in the middle of a dome-topped room bequeathed with *zellij* (ceramic tile mosaic) and gilding detail. Smaller tombs (holding his sons) sit on either side of his tomb.

Lalla Messaouda's Tomb

In the courtyard, an older mausoleum carved with blessings, and vigilantly guarded by stray cats, is the tomb built for al-Mansour's mother, Lalla Messaouda. It actually sits over an even older mausoleum, which contained the tomb of the Saadian family founder, Mohammed esh Sheikh.

The Garden Tombs

Not an alpha prince during al-Mansour's reign? Then you were relegated to the garden plot along with his wives, royal household members and some 170 chancellors. His most trusted Jewish advisers did earn pride of place in the main burial hall, though – literally closer to the king's heart than his wives.

☑ **Top Tips**

▶ The site is busy with tour groups from about 9.30am to 1pm and a long queue can form to view al-Mansour's chamber. Either get here right on opening time to admire the tombs in peace or try to come later in the day.

▶ The late afternoon is the best time for photography as the marble work takes on a golden hue in the light.

▶ The entrance is unmarked. Walk to the southern end of the Kasbah Mosque, with the Kasbah Café directly across the road, and head down the skinny alleyway.

✖ **Take a Break**

Conveniently just across the road from the entrance to the Saadian Tombs, Kasbah Café (p95) is a top spot to recharge your sightseeing batteries.

For camel burgers, date milkshakes and a fun, friendly vibe, head down Rue de la Kasbah to Cafe Clock (p91).

Top Sights
Dar Si Said

This 19th-century medina mansion was once home to Si Said, brother to Vizier Bou Ahmed of Bahia Palace fame. You can easily see the architectural and artistic similarities between the two residences, although the Dar Si Said was built on a much smaller scale. You're here to see the interiors, but it's also home to the Museum of Moroccan Arts.

Map p88, C1

0524 38 95 64

Derb Si Said

adult/child Dh10/3

9am-4.45pm Wed-Mon

Ground-Floor Galleries

The rather plain interiors of the ground-floor salons showcase Moroccan traditional crafts. On display are antique granary doors carved with talismans warding off the evil eye, a carved wooden *minbar* (mosque pulpit), rare Berber embroidery and Tuareg textiles from the 18th and 19th centuries.

Inner Courtyard

The ground-floor galleries lead out into a peaceful inner courtyard, where a central fountain sits under a wooden gazebo with an intricately painted ceiling. Bordering the courtyard, ornately decorated arched doorways lead into rooms holding collections of Berber jewellery, 19th-century armaments and Fez ceramics.

The Wedding Chamber

Climb the narrow staircase to the 1st floor to visit the spectacular painted and domed wedding-reception chamber, credited to artisans from Fez. Here musicians' balconies flank the vast main salon boasting exuberantly coloured cedar-wood ceilings. The rooms also contain exhibit cases displaying beautifully carved antique wedding chests.

Miniature Ferris Wheel

The Dar Si Said's cutest exhibit is also found in the wedding-chamber salons. Here you can see – health and safety be damned – the pint-sized palanquins that once carried babies on a miniature fairground Ferris wheel made for infants; it turned on a hand-cranked axis.

☑ **Top Tips**

▶ If you ran into tour group crowds at Bahia Palace and are regretting not spending more time admiring the painted cedar-wood ceilings and ornate plasterwork artistry, don't fret. The Dar Si Said's upstairs rooms are home to excellent examples of *zouak* work and the elaborate arched doorways of the central courtyard are worthy artistic contenders.

✗ **Take a Break**

Scoot back towards Djemaa el-Fna down Rue Riad Zitoun el-Jedid for a coffee and a sandwich at Un Déjeuner à Marrakesh (p94).

Alternatively, sample authentic Lebanese dishes at Naranj (p92).

Djemaa el-Fna

DOUAR GRAOUA

R Douar Graoua

Place de Foucauld

Kennaria
Dabachi

Place Douar Graoua

N 0   200 m
0   0.1 miles

R Moulay Ismaïl
R Bani Marine
R Bab Agnaou
R Sidi Bouloukat

R Riad Zitoun el-Kedim

R de la Recette

R Riad
el-Moukha

R Riad

Dar Si Said

RIADS ZITOUN

Maison Tiskiwin

R de la Bahia

Palais de la Bahia

Jnanie Ben Chegra

Derb Jdid

Hammam Ziani

Bahia Palace

R Imam Rhezali

Cemetery

Ave Houmane el-Fetouaki

R Ibn Rachid

R Bab Mellah

Derb Manchoura

Miâara Jewish Cemetery

Lazama Synagogue

R Uqba ben Nafaa

R Uqba ben Nafaa

Place des Ferblantiers

MELLAH

Badi Palace

KASBAH

Kasbah Mosque

Saadian Tombs

Sultana Spa

R de la Kasbah

Royal Palace

Bab Ksiba

R du Mechouar

Les Jardins de la Medina

Agdal Gardens

For reviews see	
Top Sights	p82
Sights	p89
Eating	p91
Drinking	p95
Shopping	p97

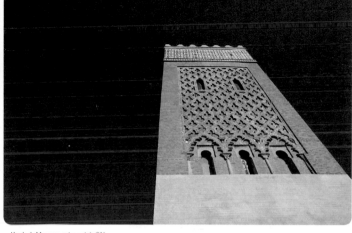

DCLLYTH-DOG/SHUTTERSTOCK ©

Kasbah Mosque minaret (p91)

Sights

Badi Palace
HISTORIC SITE

1 ◎ Map p88, B3

As 16th-century sultan Ahmed al-Mansour was paving the Badi Palace with gold, turquoise and crystal, his court jester wisecracked, 'It'll make a beautiful ruin.' That jester was no fool: 75 years later the place was looted and today only remnants remain. El-Badi's vast courtyard, with its four sunken gardens and reflecting pools, give a hint of the palace's former majesty and the views from the pisé ramparts, where storks nest, are magnificent. (Behind Pl des Ferblantiers; adult/child Dh10/3, Koutoubia minbar extra Dh10; ⊙9am-5pm)

Maison Tiskiwin
MUSEUM

2 ◎ Map p88, C2

Travel to Timbuktu and back again via Dutch anthropologist Bert Flint's art collection, displayed at Maison Tiskiwin. Each room represents a caravan stop along the Sahara-to-Marrakesh route, presenting indigenous crafts from Tuareg camel saddles to High Atlas carpets. The accompanying text is often more eccentric than explanatory, but Tiskiwin's well-travelled artefacts offer tantalising glimpses of Marrakesh's trading-post past. (☑0524 38 91 92; www.tiskiwin.com; 8 Rue de la Bahia; adult/child Dh20/10; ⊙9.30am-12.30pm & 2.30-6pm)

Top Tip

The Koutoubia Minbar

Don't scrimp on your ticket at Badi Palace (p89): the main attraction in the ruins (if you don't count the awesome rampart views) is the Koutoubia *minbar* (prayer pulpit) and it's well worth the additional Dh10 entry fee. Once the *minbar* of the Koutoubia Mosque, its cedarwood steps with gold and silver calligraphy were the work of 12th-century Cordoban artisans headed by a man named Aziz – the Metropolitan Museum of Art restoration surfaced his signature.

Lazama Synagogue   SYNAGOGUE

 3 Map p88, C3

In the *mellah* (Jewish quarter), the Lazama Synagogue is still used by Marrakesh's dwindling Jewish community. A nondescript door leads into a pretty blue-and-white courtyard with the synagogue on the right-hand side. Inside the austere worship area, note the *zellij* tilework's Star of David motif. The courtyard's surrounding ground-floor rooms have exhibits of Moroccan Jewish life. (Derb Manchoura; Dh10; ⏰9am-5pm Sun-Thu, 9am-1pm Fri, closed Jewish holidays)

Miaâra Jewish Cemetery   CEMETERY

4 Map p88, D2

In this sprawling walled cemetery, the exceptionally helpful gatekeeper admits visitors who wish to pay

their respects to whitewashed tombs topped with rocks for remembrance. (Rue el-Miaâra; entry by Dh10 donation; ⏰Sun-Thu 9am-5pm, Fri 8am-1pm, closed Jewish holidays)

Sultana Spa   HAMMAM

 5 Map p88, A4

An opulent, all-marble spa near the Saadian Tombs offering services from a basic hammam experience to pampering massages (Dh600 to Dh1400), signature cinnamon body scrubs and facial treatments using argan and prickly-pear oils. (📞0524 38 80 08; www.lasultanamarrakech.com; Rue de la Kasbah; hammam & gommage Dh400)

Hammam Ziani   HAMMAM

 6 Map p88, C2

Not ready for the real-deal public hammams, but don't want the European spa treatment? Hammam Ziani is a happy compromise. There are lockers for your bags and clothes; the tea-drinking room is decked out like a highly kitsch Orientalist fantasy; and the friendly masseurs will scrub and pummel you into total relaxation. (📞0662 71 55 71; www.hammamziani.ma; 14 Rue Riad Zitoun el-Jedid; hammam & gommage Dh120; ⏰8am-10pm)

Les Jardins de la Medina   SWIMMING

 7 Map p88, B5

This 19th-century palace-cum-boutique hotel is the most beautiful place in the medina for a light lunch and an afternoon of poolside lounging. The huge riad garden is planted with old palms, orange and olive trees, and jacarandas that burst into dramatic blue bloom in early summer. Nonguests must have lunch (mains Dh100 to Dh180) to access the pool. Advance reservation is required. (0524 38 18 51; www.lesjardinsdelamedina. com; Derb Chtouka 21; pool pass Dh100)

Kasbah Mosque MOSQUE

8 Map p88, A3

Built in 1190, the Kasbah Mosque is the main mosque for the southern end of the medina. If you were wondering what Marrakesh's famed Koutoubia Minaret would have looked like when it was covered in pink plaster, the mosque's pastel-pink minaret gives you a fair idea. (Pl des Saadians; closed to non-Muslims)

Eating

Dar Anika MOROCCAN $$$

9 Map p88, B2

The small terrace, framed by palms and trailing bougainvillea, is all about romantic candlelit dining. The main courses offer a tastebud tour of Moroccan dishes often missing from medina menus. For a sweet-savoury kick order the chicken *seffa medfouna* (chicken topped with raisin, almond and cinnamon spiked vermicelli) or go full-hog and pre-order (four hours in

Local Life
The Mellah

To experience a less bustling corner of the medina and capture a sense of Marrakesh's once-vibrant Jewish community, head to the *mellah* (Jewish quarter). Here, amid the narrow *derbs* (alleys) are the tallest mudbrick buildings in Marrakesh. Most Jewish families moved away in the 1960s, but the *mellah* remains notable for its mudbrick homes set along narrow streets where cross-alley gossip can be whispered through wrought-iron balconies.

advance) the camel *tanjia*. (0524 39 17 51; www.riaddaranika.com; 112 Riad Zitoun el-Kedim; mains Dh150-200; 11.30am-2.30pm & 6.30-11pm)

Cafe Clock CAFE $$

10 Map p88, B5

Little sister to the Fez original, Cafe Clock is housed in an old school with sunset views over the Kasbah. The signature camel burger, inventive sandwiches and salads are reason enough to drop in, but the cross-cultural vibe

Local Life
Cheap Eats

Rue de la Kasbah is prime territory for cheap and cheerful meals, with Marrakshis flocking to the *snaks* (kiosks) and cubby-hole restaurants for a quick no-fuss, no-frills lunch.

LIGHTKEY/GETTY IMAGES ©

Badi Palace (p89)

will keep you returning. Every Monday and Thursday it hosts traditional *hikayat* (storytelling) performances and there's live Gnaoua and Amazigh music on Sundays. (📞0524 37 83 67; www.cafeclock.com; 224 Derb Chtouka; mains Dh60-95; 🕙10am-10pm; 🛜🖊)

PepeNero
ITALIAN, MOROCCAN $$$

11 🍽 Map p88, C1

Housed in part of Riad al Moussika, Thami el Glaoui's one-time pleasure palace, this Italian-Moroccan restaurant is one of the finest in the medina, with its fresh house-made pasta stealing the show. Request a table beside the courtyard pool, rimmed by citrus trees, to make the most of the occasion. Reservations required. (📞0524 38 90 67; www.pepenero-marrakech.com; 17 Derb Cherkaoui; mains Dh120-220, 3-course lunch menu Dh190; 🕙12.30-2.30pm & 7.30-11pm Tue-Sun; 🛜🖊)

Naranj
LEBANESE $$

12 🍽 Map p88, B1

If you know your felafel from your fattoush make a beeline here. Inside it's a glam mix of funky *khamsa* mirrors, low-hanging copper lamps and stripy textiles that wouldn't be out of place in a hipster Beirut cafe. Which is the point, because the menu is of bang-on classic Lebanese favourites with a couple of contemporary twists. (📞0524 38 68 05; www.naranj.ma; 84 Rue Riad Zitoun el-Jedid; mains Dh69-119; 🕙11am-11pm; 🚭❄)

Understand
Moroccan Tunes

Morocco's indigenous music traditions fall into three main categories, with contemporary musicians often blending both modern and traditional styles.

If you're in the kasbah area during the evening, swing on by to Cafe Clock (p91), which hosts live music four nights a week. This is a great opportunity to see local musicians. Saturday nights are dedicated to Berber folk and a Gnaoua band plays on Sundays.

Berber Folk

The oldest musical traditions in Morocco are Berber, and there are a variety of different forms that have evolved from the various Berber tribes. This music is usually distinctive for its chanting formula, set to a simple beat.

Gnaoua

Joyously bluesy, with a rhythm you can't refuse, Gnaoua began among freed slaves as a ritual of deliverance from slavery and into God's graces. Don't be surprised if the beat sends you into a trance – that's what it's meant to do. A true Gnaoua *lila* (spiritual jam session) may last all night, with musicians erupting into leaps of joy as they enter trance-like states of ecstasy.

Arab-Andalucian

Leaving aside the thorny question of where it actually originated (you don't want to be the cause of the next centuries-long Spain–Morocco conflict, do you?), this music combines the flamenco-style strumming and heart-string-plucking drama of Spanish folk music with the finely calibrated stringed-instruments, complex percussion and haunting half-tones of classical Arab music.

Modern Moroccan

Like the rest of the Arab world, Moroccans listen to a lot of Egyptian music but they also have their own home-grown Moroccan pop, rock and hip-hop (called *hibhub*). Although cherry-picking influences from the international scene, many Moroccan bands and singers manage to fuse elements of Gnaoua and Berber folk into their sound to fashion a musical style that is purely Moroccan.

Un Déjeuner à Marrakech

MEDITERRANEAN $$

13 Map p88, B1

Popular with the lunching crowd, Un Déjeuner dishes up a Mediterranean menu that jumps from Tangier shrimp to steak, mozzarella salad and pumpkin balls. The cactus-lined roof terrace is the place to be on a blue-skied, breezy Moroccan spring day. (📞0524 37 83 87; 2-4 Rue Riad Zitoun el-Jedid, cnr Douar Graoua; mains Dh85-135; ⏰11am-10pm; ❄🛜🍴)

✓ Top Tip

Street Food

Enjoy street food and stay healthy with the following tips:

▶ Make a beeline for busy stores: Marrakshis are sticklers for freshness and know which places consistently deliver.

▶ Look over the ingredients and check the food on display, especially if ordering meat or seafood.

▶ Clean your hands before eating. Much of what we call 'food poisoning' is actually illness caused by bacteria transferred from hand to mouth while eating.

▶ Use bread to scoop up food. This is how Moroccans eat and it makes sense. Utensils are usually only briefly rinsed in cold water so not your best bet hygiene-wise.

La Table al Badia

MOROCCAN $$$

14 Map p88, C3

This highly atmospheric riad is a top choice for Moroccan cooking, with *dada* (chef) Samira at the control deck serving up her own take on the country's classics. Produce is bought from the market each day, so everything's as fresh and tasty as you can get. Reservations are essential. For the best seats, reserve a table on the rooftop. (📞0524 39 01 10; www.riadal badia.com; Riad al-Badia, 135 Derb ahl Souss; 3-course set dinner Dh200; ⏰from 7pm)

Fox Art Food

CAFE $

15 Map p88, B2

Overseen by the fox-headed mannequin out front, this funky, fun cafe is run by a group of local artists as a means to support their work. Pull up a stool (made from old crates and recycled denim) and order lunch from the small menu that trips from sandwiches, salads and burgers to a couple of tajine offerings. (Riad Zitoun el-Kedim; mains Dh35-50; ⏰11am-10pm; 😊)

Snack Essaidiyne

MOROCCAN $

16 Map p88, A4

No fuss. No frills. Just a couple of plastic tables and some skewered meat char-grilled to perfection. For the royal sum of Dh30 you get six skewers of meat (choose from lamb, chicken, *kefta* or liver), a dish of olives and some bread. Side dishes of salads and chips are an extra Dh10. (Rue de la Kasbah; meals Dh30–40; ⏰10am-10pm)

Restaurant Place Ferblantiers No 8 · MOROCCAN $

17 🍴 Map p88, B3

Plop down on a plastic chair out front and have whatever's well caramelised and bubbling away on the burner. One of a line of restaurants dishing up the same menu on this side of Place des Ferblantiers, No 8 is a friendly, solid choice for cheap and cheerful tajines. (Pl des Ferblantiers; tajines Dh35-45; ⏰10am-7pm)

Drinking

Kosybar · BAR

18 🍷 Map p88, C3

The Marrakesh-meets-Kyoto interiors are full of plush, private nooks, but keep heading upstairs to low-slung canvas sofas on the rooftop terrace where storks give cocktail-sippers the once-over from nearby nests. Skip the cardboard-esque sushi and stick with the bar snacks. (📞0524 38 03 24; http:// kozibar.tripod.com; 4/ Pl des Ferblantiers; ⏰noon-1am; ✳🛜)

Kasbah Café · CAFE

19 🍷 Map p88, A3

Say hello to your neighbours, the beak-clacking storks perched on the Saadian Tombs, and then relax with a fresh juice, milkshake or mint tea. For

Top Tip

Taking a Taxi

It's quite a hike between the kasbah area of the medina and the ville nouvelle so you may want to use a taxi.

All *petits taxis* (local taxis) are supposed to use a meter. Unfortunately someone forgot to send the drivers this memo.

▶ To ask in French for the meter to be switched on, say '*tourne lecon-teur, si'l vous plaît*'.

▶ If the driver refuses and is quoting a ridiculous price, ask to stop and get out.

▶ Hail off the street. Taxis milling in ranks are usually the worst offenders.

▶ Don't get upset. Marrakesh taxis are notorious for overcharging visitors. It's not worth ruining your day over.

sunset views over the *mellah*, arrive between 6.30pm and 7pm. There are pizzas, and *brochette* (kebab) skewers dangling on a stand as well (📞0524 38 26 25; 47 Boutouil; ⏰8am-10pm; ✳🛜)

La Porte du Monde · CAFE

20 🍷 Map p88, B1

At this place, tucked into the corner of Rue Riad Zitoun el-Jedid, choose either a comfy wicker-style chair at street level or escape the souq mayhem on the terrace, decorated with

Understand
Medina Architecture 101

Medinas have their own distinctive urban layout and forms of architecture. The twisty labyrinth of alleyways will keep you wondering what's behind that wall or down that block. The following are some of the most common medina features you'll see:

Kasbahs
This extra fortified quarter housed the ruling family and all the necessities for living in case of a siege. Marrakesh's 11th-century kasbah is one of the largest remaining in Morocco and still houses a royal palace.

Ramparts
The Almoravids wrapped Marrakesh in 16km of pink pisé (rammed earth) walls, 2m thick. These dramatic and defensive walls still separate the medina from the ville nouvelle today.

Religious Buildings
Non-Muslims cannot enter any of the mosques in Marrakesh but are able to admire the striking minarets from outside. Marrakesh also has seven *zawiyas* (shrines to a *marabout* – saint). You'll recognise these by their green ceramic-tiled roofs.

Riads
So many riads have become hotels in recent years that the word has become a synonym for 'guesthouse' but, technically, an authentic riad has a courtyard garden divided in four parts, with a fountain in the centre.

Souqs & Qissariat
Souqs are the medina's market streets. They're criss-crossed with smaller streets lined with storerooms and cubby-hole-sized artisans' studios. Unlike souqs, these smaller streets often do not have names, and are together known as a *qissariat*. Most *qissaria* are through-streets, so when (not if) you get lost in them, keep heading onward until you intersect with the next souq – or buy a carpet, whichever happens first.

eclectic art and colourful wrought iron. It's a chilled-out spot to relax with a tea or coffee; if you're peckish there's a menu of couscous, tajines and grills. (Rue Riad Zitoun el-Jedid; ⊙10.30am-10pm)

Café Table de Marrakech   CAFE

21 🚍 Map p88, C2

Stagger up the stairs after sightseeing and plonk yourself down at one of the rooftop tables overlooking the entry to Bahia Palace. The food here is nothing to write home about, but it's a prime position to recuperate with a fruit juice or a pot of tea. (Rue Riad Zitoun el-Jedid; ⊙10.30am-11pm)

Shopping

Naturom   COSMETICS

22 🔒 Map p88, B2

There are lots of things to like about Naturom, not least its 100% organic certification and the use of pure essences and essential oils (argan, avocado, wheat germ), which ensure that all of its beauty products are completely hypo-allergenic. And with its own medicinal and herbal garden, Naturom offers full traceability of all raw materials. (📞0673 46 02 09; 213 Rue Riad Zitoun el-Jedid; ⊙9.30am-8pm Sat-Thu, to noon Fri)

Moroccan mint tea

Creations Pneumatiques
ARTS & CRAFTS

23 Map p88, B2

To buy crafts directly from Marrakesh's recycling artisans, head over to Riad Zitoun el-Kedim and check out lanterns, bowls and belts cleverly fashioned from tin cans and tyres. There are several to choose from, but this place (look for the framed Bob Marley poster) has a good selection of Michelin mirrors, inner-tube jewellery boxes, and man-bags with street cred. (110 Rue Riad Zitoun el-Kedim; ⏱10am-7pm)

Metalworker Stalls
HOMEWARES

24 🔒 Map p88, C3

Place des Ferblantiers (Tinsmith Square) has recently received a modern revamp by the local council but its traditional use, as a home to metal-worker stalls, has thankfully been upheld. It's a good place to browse through a mammoth array of lanterns and funky metal lampshades. (Pl des Ferblantiers; ⏱10am-7pm)

Jamade
ARTS & CRAFTS

25 🔒 Map p88, B1

A stand-out collection of locally designed items at fixed prices. Recent scores include graphite ceramic olive-oil cruets, breezy ice-blue linen tunics, citrus-seed bead necklaces with a clever antique-coin closure, and hip, hand-sewn coasters from the Tigmi women's cooperative. (📞0524 42 90 42; 1 Pl Douar Graoua, cnr Rue Riad Zitoun el-Jedid; ⏱10am-noon & 3-7.30pm)

Understand
Moroccan Social Graces

Many visitors are surprised at how quickly friendships can be formed in Marrakesh, and are often a little suspicious. True, carpet dealers aren't after your friendship when they offer you mint tea, but notice how Moroccans behave with one another and you'll see that friendly overtures are more than a mere contrivance.

People you meet in passing are likely to remember you and greet you warmly the next day, and it's considered polite to stop and ask how they're doing. Greetings among friends can last 10 minutes as each person enquires after the other's happiness, wellbeing and family. Moroccans are generous with their time and extend courtesies that might seem to you like impositions, from walking you to your next destination to inviting you home for lunch. To show your appreciation for the latter, stop by the next day to say hello and be sure to compliment the cook.

Spices and soaps for sale, Mellah Market

Mellah Market
MARKET

26 🔒 Map p88, B3

For the south side of the city, this is a major source of food, flowers and other household goods. Fair warning to vegetarians: the door closest to Place des Ferblantiers leads directly to the butchery stalls where carcasses swing next to clucking chickens and caged rabbits. (Ave Houmane el-Fetouaki; 🕙8am-1pm & 3-7pm)

Grand Bijouterie
JEWELLERY

27 🔒 Map p88, B2

This tiny jeweller's souq is a legacy of the Jewish artisans of the *mellah*. Gold is still sold by weight here and some stores still specialise in locally made fine filigree work. (Rue Bab Mellah; 🕙9am-7pm)

Explore

Ville Nouvelle

Need a break from the medina hustle? Head to Marrakesh's ville nouvelle (new town), full of leafy parks, cafe culture, a thriving contemporary art scene and the best bars and gourmet restaurants in town. Guéliz is the central shopping hub, while Hivernage is a high-class neighbourhood bordered by gardens and home to a few remnants of art deco architecture.

The Sights in a Day

☀️ Catch modern Marrakesh at work by strolling through the centre of Guéliz. Sit down for a pot of tea or a coffee and soak up the old-world vibe at **Grand Café de la Poste** (p114) and then check out the Orientalist art works on show at **MACMA** (p108).

☀️ Sample a slap-up feast of Moroccan homestyle cooking for lunch at the **Amal Center** (p109) before heading up to **Jardin Majorelle** (p102) to wander around Yves Saint Laurent's old stomping ground. Don't forget to visit the beautifully curated collection of the **Musée Berbère** (p103) while here, to brush up on the fascinating culture of Morocco's Amazigh peoples.

🌙 Dinner decisions are tough in Guéliz. For the best of the city's Moroccan cuisine, dine at **Al Fassia** (p110) – don't forget to book – or, if you're hankering for a cuisine change, get a table at **Catanzaro** (p110) for real-deal Italian pizza. Finish off with a drink at lively **68 Bar à Vin** (p114).

For a local's day of gallery-hopping in Guéliz, see p104.

 Top Sights

Jardin Majorelle (p102)

🔍 **Local Life**

Guéliz Gallery Hop (p104)

❤️ **Best of Marrakesh**

Food
Amal Center (p109)
Al Fassia (p110)
Snack al-Bahriya (p113)
Pâtisserie Amandine (p110)
Panna Gelato (p109)

Arts & Crafts
MACMA (p108)
Galerie Rê (p105)

Berber Culture
Musée Berbère (p103)

Getting There

🚖 **Taxi** It shouldn't cost more than Dh20 between Djemaa el-Fna and central Guéliz.

🚶 **Walk** It's a 20- to 25-minute stroll from Djemaa el-Fna to Guéliz, straight up Ave Mohammed V.

🚌 **Bus** Buses 1 and 16 head to Guéliz. Catch them from the bus stop on Place de Foucauld, near Djemaa el-Fna.

Top Sights
Jardin Majorelle

Yves Saint Laurent gifted the Jardin Majorelle to Marrakesh, the city he fell in love with in 1966. Saint Laurent and his partner, Pierre Bergé, bought the garden in 1980 to preserve the vision of its original owner, landscape painter Jacques Majorelle. Today it remains a psychedelic desert mirage of 300 plant species from five continents.

◉ Map p106, D2

☏ 0524 31 30 47

www.jardinmajorelle.com

cnr Aves Yacoub el-Mansour & Moulay Abdullah

adult/child Dh70/free

🕗 8am-6pm, to 5.30pm Oct-Apr

Former studio of Jacques Majorelle, now home to Musée Berbère

Musée Berbère

Majorelle's electric-blue art deco studio houses the fabulous **Musée Berbère** (adult/child Dh30/free; ⊘8am-6pm, to 5.30pm Oct-Apr), which showcases the rich panorama of Morocco's indigenous inhabitants in displays of some 600 artefacts, including wood and metalwork, textiles and a stunning display of regional traditional costumes. Best of all is the mirrored chamber displaying a collection of chiselled, filigreed and enamelled jewels.

Garden Strolls

This has to be one of the most serene spots in the city. A circular walking path weaves between bamboo groves, palm trees and cactus gardens leading to ponds looked over by a highly ornamental pavilion. A series of signs along the path describes the plants in each garden.

Getting Blue with Majorelle

The blue used abundantly throughout the garden – most famously on the studio's exterior – is known as Majorelle blue and makes a zany contrast set against all that greenery. Supposedly Majorelle mixed this particular tint so that it would match the blue overalls that French workmen wear, though we've never seen workmen look quite this snazzy.

Yves Saint Laurent Mementoes

The Galerie Love displays Yves Saint Laurent's 'Love Posters', which favoured clients of the fashion house received every New Year. In the eastern garden section is the memorial to the man himself. His ashes were scattered here after his death in 2008. A YSL museum is scheduled to open in the garden in late 2017.

☑ **Top Tips**

▶ The afternoon is the best time for keen photographers to get the prettiest light for their snaps.

▶ Don't scrimp the extra Dh30 and miss the Musée Berbère. Its exhibits are by far the best curated in Marrakesh and well worth the cost.

▶ The taxi drivers who hang out around Jardin Majorelle are renowned for overcharging. Walk a bit further down Ave Yacoub el Mansour and hail a taxi off the road – or prepare to pay way over the odds for your ride.

✕ **Take a Break**

Right inside the gardens themselves, Café Majorelle serves up juices and crunchy salads on a shady terrace surrounded by greenery.

A hop, skip and jump from the exit is Kaowa (p115), where you can slurp down a healthy smoothie to beat the heat.

Local Life
Guéliz Gallery Hop

Marrakesh's tourist art market may still trade in an exotic mishmash of harem girls, men with muskets and other Orientalist clichés, but in the ville nouvelle district of Guéliz an entire new generation of Marrakshi artists are spreading their wings and offering up original talent. Explore the city's contemporary art scene to see how Marrakesh is moving with the times.

1 An Arty Alley

Start off at the Passage Ghandouri, a tiny alleyway home to a number of small private galleries. Here you'll find the **Matisse Art Gallery** (☑0524 44 83 26; www.matisseartgallery.com; 43 Passage Ghandouri; ⏱9.30am-noon & 3-7.30pm Mon-Sat), where previously local artists such as Aziz Abou Ali and Mahi Binebine have shown their work.

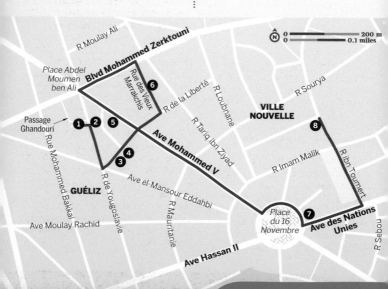

2 Moroccan Movers & Shakers

Hop across the road to **Galerie Noir sur Blanc** (📞0524 42 24 10, www.galerienoirsur blanc.com; 1st fl, 48 Rue de Yougoslavie; ⏰3-7pm Mon, 10am-1pm & 3-7pm Tue-Sat) where a permanent exhibit of Moroccan talent is complemented by temporary exhibits focused on local artists. The well-informed staff here can provide useful insights into the local art scene.

3 Hang Out at Kechmara

Join Guéliz's hip brigade and kick back with a coffee at **Kechmara** (📞0524 42 25 32; www.kechmara.com; 3 Rue de La Liberté; ⏰11.30am-1am Mon-Sat; ❄🛜) where the daytime soundtrack is cool-jazz, the coffee is strong and the walls play host to a series of changing modern art exhibitions. For the peckish, there's a menu of steaks, burgers and salads.

4 A Sweet-Tooth's Stop

Drop into **Patisserie Al-Jawda** (📞0524 43 38 97; 11 Rue de la Liberté; ⏰8am-7.30pm) for dessert. This Guéliz institution is one of the best places in town to sample traditional Moroccan sweets featuring figs, orange-flower water, desert honey and other local, seasonal ingredients.

5 Check Out Some Snaps

Move on to **Gallery 127** (📞0524 43 26 67; www.galerienathalielocatelli.com; 2nd fl, 127 Ave Mohammed V; ⏰2-7pm Tue-Sat), found by taking a once-grand stairway up to the industrial-chic art space. The gallery exhibits a range of new and vintage works (from straightforward travel

photography to more interpretive) by international photographers at reasonable prices. Afterwards, visit bustling Blvd Mohamed Zerktouni to capture a sense of modern Marrakesh at work.

6 Dive into an Abstract World

In the **David Bloch Gallery** (📞0524 45 75 95; www.davidblochgallery.com; 8 bis Rue des Vieux Marrakchis; ⏰10.30am-1.30pm & 3.30-7.30pm Tue-Sat, 3.30-7.30pm Mon) artists from both sides of the Mediterranean strike fine lines between traditional calligraphy and urban graffiti in a series of temporary exhibitions. Here, you can catch the work of the scene's young up-and-coming abstract artists.

7 Snack at Café 16

Nab an outdoor table at **Café 16** (📞0524 33 96 70; 18 Pl du 16 Novembre; desserts Dh70, sandwiches & salads Dh120-140; ⏰9am-midnight), which blends European style with a warm Marrakshi welcome. Have a light salad or sandwich snack then dig into the intriguing ice-cream flavours, such as mint tea and *kaab el-gazelle* (almond cookie) or treat yourself to the divine raspberry mousse cake.

8 View the Next Big Thing

To finish off, check out the next generation of Moroccan art stars at **Galerie Rê** (📞0524 43 22 58; www.galeriere.com; Résidence Al Andalous III, cnr Rues de la Mosquée & Ibn Toumert; ⏰10am-1pm & 3-8pm Mon-Sat). Both the permanent and temporary galleries at this super suave space host a wealth of emerging talent from across North Africa.

Ave du 11 Janvier

Blvd Allal el-Fassi

BAB DOUKKALA & DAR EL-BACHA

R Bab Doukkala

Bab Doukkala

Jardin Majorelle

30
19
27

Ave Moulay Abdullah

R Khalid ben el-Oualid

Oum Errabia

Ave des Nations Unies

R Sebou

Ave Yacoub el-Mansour

VILLE NOUVELLE

R ibn Toumert

Place du 16 Novembre

R Souriya

R ibn Malik

23

Office National Marocain du Tourisme

R Loubnane

16
21
8

R Liberte

R Tariq Ibn Ziyad

Ave Mohammed V

17

R Mauritanie

22

R ben Ali

29

11
7

Place Abdel Moumen

R de Yougoslavie

14

26

1

10

9

Ave el-Mansour Eddahbi

GUÉLIZ

MACMA

6

R ibn Sina

18

13

15

21

R Moulay Ali

20

R ibn Aïcha

Polyclinique du Sud

R ibn Zaïdoun

R Abdelouahab Derraq

31

12

Ave Abdelkrim el-Khattabi

Blvd Mohammed Zerktouni

Ave Moulay Rachid

R el-Hassan ben N'Bar

Marrakesh Train Station

Ave Mohammed VI

For reviews see

◉	Top Sights	p102
◎	Sights	p108
✕	Eating	p109
✕	Drinking	p114
✕	Entertainment	p116
✕	Shopping	p116

A B C D E
1 2 3 4

28

2
CyberPark

Le Mamounia
Gardens
4

Ave Bab Jedid

Bab
Nkob

Ave el-Yarmouk

R Abbès Sebti

R Haroun
Errachid

Bab el-
Jedid

Place de la
Liberté

Ave Echouhada

R Haroun Errachid

25

R de Paris

R Ibrahim el Mazini

Ave de la Menara

e Yacoub al-Marini

R Moulay el Hassan

24

HIVERNAGE

R el-Qadissa

R Oudi e
Makhazin

R de Paris

5
Jardin
Harti

Ave du Président Kennedy

Ave Mohammed VI

yad
Theatre
Royal R el-Qadi A

3

R Abou Bakr Seddiq

CTM Bus
Station

R el-Jahed

Ave Hassan II

500 m
0.25 miles

N

A
B
C
D
E

5
6
7
8

Sights

MACMA
GALLERY

1  Map p106, B3

It may be small but the big guns of Orientalist painting are all on display at this suave gallery, opened in early 2016. The impressive collection of 19th- and 20th-century works by European artists who fell for Morocco's landscapes and peoples includes those by Henri Le Riche, Edy Legrand, Roger Marcel Limouse and, of course, Jacques Majorelle – he of garden fame (p102). (Musee d'Art et de Culture de Marrakech; ☎0524 44 83 26; 61 Passage Ghandouri, Rue de Yougoslavie; adult/student Dh40/20; ⏱10am-7pm Mon-Sat)

CyberPark
GARDENS

2  Map p106, E6

Stop and smell the roses at this 8-hectare royal garden, dating from the 18th century. It now offers free wi-fi at outdoor kiosks and an air-conditioned cybercafe (Dh10 per hour) – hence the park's less-than-regal name. This garden is a well-maintained and shady retreat, popular with young couples and early-evening strollers. (Ave Mohammed V; admission free; ⏱9am-7pm)

Theatre Royal
ARCHITECTURE

3  Map p106, B5

Begun in the 1970s by Tunisian architect Charles Boccara, this grand edifice is still unfinished. If the front

GIMAS/GETTY IMAGES ©

Theatre Royal

door's open, pop your head in, as the caretaker may offer to show you around, for a tip. If so, check out the domed ceiling, brickwork detailing and woodwork flourishes that merge Moroccan and European styles, and the huge unfinished opera house. (Ave Hassan II, Guéliz; admission free)

La Mamounia Gardens
GARDENS

6 Map p106, E7

On their trips to Marrakesh, Winston Churchill and Franklin D Roosevelt spent their downtime here, among the rose bushes and ornamental shrubbery that belong to the luxurious La Mamounia Hotel. These days the garden isn't as elegantly kept up as it must have been in its glory days, but it's still a relaxing spot to get away from the hurly-burly of the city. Don't dress too scruffily if you want the doorstaff at the hotel gate to let you in. (Ave Houmane el Fetouaki; admission free)

Jardin Harti
PARK

5 Map p106, C5

Slap in the centre of Guéliz, this tranquil park is full of palm-tree-shaded benches and flower beds that bloom through summer. The two rather tatty life-sized dinosaurs also make it a favourite hang-out for local families out for a weekend stroll. (Rue Ouadi el-Makhazine; admission free; ⏰8am-6pm)

Eating

Amal Center
MOROCCAN $

6 Map p106, B2

Do good while eating delicious food – double bonus. The Amal Center supports and trains disadvantaged Moroccan women in restaurant skills and you get to feast on their flavours. So many Marrakesh restaurants are a poor reflection of local cuisine, but here you get the real home-cooking deal. On our last visit we had the best

---

Local Life

Ice Cream

When the mercury heads above 40°C, in Marrakesh, ice cream isn't a treat – it's a staple. Unsurprisingly there are plenty of places to get a cone.

If you're near the train station, **Venezia Ice** (Map p106, A4; Ave Mohammed VI; scoop Dh16; ⏰9am-10pm) sells ice creams and tangy sorbets made by a Casablanca-based company.

But the city's most famous ice-cream parlour is **Panna Gelato** (Map p106, A2; ☎0524 43 65 65; www.pannagelaoitaliano.it; cnr Rue du Capitaine Arrigui & Ave Mohammed V; cone Dh20; ⏰7.30am-10pm; ❄). Created by a master gelato artisan from Italy, with proprietary recipes using fine local ingredients, it's worth the troop (or taxi ride) up Ave Mohammed V just for a scoop.

Local Life

Weekday Lunches

At weekday lunchtimes local office workers descend in droves on the string of restaurants along **Rue Mohammed Bakkal** in Guéliz to refuel on grilled meat goodness, well-caramelised tajines and offal offerings. Grab a table at whichever restaurant you fancy and join in.

Our favourite is **Plats Haj Boujemaa** (Map p106, A2; 65 Rue Mohammed Bakkal; mains Dh25-45; ⊙noon-10pm Tue-Sun). This unpretentious place covers all the bases with pizza, pasta and steak thrown in, too, but what it's known for is its perfectly grilled *brochettes*.

fish tajine we've ever tasted in Morocco. (☑0524 44 68 96; amalnonprofit.org; cnr Rues Allal ben Ahmad & Ibn Sina; mains Dh50-60; ⊙noon-4pm)

Al Fassia
MOROCCAN $$$

7 Map p106, B3

In business since 1987, this stalwart of Marrakesh's dining scene is still one of the best. Meals begin with a bang with complimentary 12-dish *mezze* (salads) while Moroccan mains of chicken tajine with caramelised pumpkin, and lamb tajine with almonds and eggs – served by an all-female waiter crew – show how the classics should be done. Reservations essential. (☑0524 43 40 60; www.alfassia.com; 55 Blvd Mohammed Zerktouni; mains Dh110-175; ⊙noon-2.30pm & 7.30-11pm Wed-Mon)

Catanzaro
ITALIAN $$

8 Map p106, C3

This is the best pizza in Morocco. It may even be the best pizza this side of the Med. We realise that's an awfully big call and maybe the very reasonably priced wine here (from Dh160 per bottle) went to our head, but Catanzaro's thin-crust, wood-fired creations (particularly the Neapolitan with capers, local olives and Atlantic anchovies) are a show-stealer. (☑0524 43 37 31; 42 Rue Tariq ibn Ziyad; mains Dh50-120; ⊙noon-2.30pm & 7.15-11pm Mon-Sat; ⊝❄)

Pâtisserie Amandine
SWEETS $

9 Map p106, B4

We need saving from places like the Amandine, with its rich custard *millefeuille*, rainbow macarons, zesty lemon tarts and delectable raspberry panna cotta pots. Our dentist thanks you in advance. (☑0524 44 96 12; www.amandine marrakech.com; 177 Rue Mohamed El Beqal; sweets & desserts from Dh10; ⊙7am-9pm; ❄)

Mamma Mia
ITALIAN $$

10 Map p106, B3

Full hat-tip to this family-friendly trattoria for its smoke-free section. Take a tajine-break and join the punters chowing down on good-value pizzas, generous bowls of pasta or main dishes of veal escalope and steak. Beer and wine are available and there's a full bar out the back (in the smoking section). (☑0524 43 44 54; www.restaurant-mammamia.com; 18 Rue de la Liberté; mains Dh50-170; ⊙10am-10pm; ⊝❄☑)

Understand

Moroccan Menu Decoder

- -

Let's get one thing straight. Moroccan cuisine is more than tajines and couscous, though you'll find these in abundance. Decode those sometimes rather befuddling Marrakesh menus with the list of popular dishes below.

Savoury Specialities

Beghrir Pancakes with a spongy crumpet-like texture. Usually served for breakfast.

Bessara Broad beans with cumin, paprika, olive oil and salt.

Briouat Cigar-shaped or triangular pastry stuffed with herbs and goat's cheese, meats or egg, then fried or baked.

Harira A hearty soup with a base of tomatoes, onions, saffron and coriander, often with lentils, chickpeas and/or lamb.

Kwa Grilled liver kebabs with cumin, salt and paprika.

Pastilla Savoury-sweet pie made of *warqa* (filo-like pastry) layered with pigeon or chicken, cooked with caramelised onions, lemon, eggs and toasted sugared almonds, then dusted with cinnamon and powdered sugar.

Sfenj Doughnuts (sometimes with an egg deep-fried in the hole).

Tajine The famous Moroccan stew cooked in a conical earthenware pot. Classic options are *dujaj mqalli bil hamd markd wa zeetoun* (chicken with preserved lemon and olives), *ketta bil matisha wa bayd* (meatballs in a rich tomato sauce, topped with a sizzling egg), and *lehem bil berquq wa luz* (lamb with prunes and almonds served in a saffron-onion sauce).

Tanjia Crockpot stew of seasoned lamb and preserved lemon, cooked for eight hours in the fire of a hammam.

Sweet Treats

Kaab el-ghazal Crescent-shaped 'gazelle's horns' cookie stuffed with almond paste and laced with orange-flower water.

Orange á canelle Orange slices with cinnamon and orange-flower water.

Sfaa Sweet cinnamon couscous with dried fruit and nuts, served with cream.

> ### Understand
> ## The Making of the Ville Nouvelle
>
> When Morocco came under colonial control, *villes nouvelles* (new towns) were built outside the walls of old city medinas, with street grids and modern architecture imposing strict order. Neoclassical facades, mansard roofs and high-rises must have come as quite a shock when they were introduced by the French. But one style that seemed to bridge local Islamic geometry and streamlined European modernism was art deco.
>
> Painter Jacques Majorelle brought a Moroccan colour sensibility to art deco in 1924, adding bursts of blue, green and acid yellow to his villa and Jardin Majorelle. In the 1930s architects began cleverly grafting Moroccan geometric detail onto whitewashed European edifices, creating a signature Moroccan art deco style that became known as Mauresque-deco. You can still see elements of this style in many of the older buildings in Marrakesh's ville nouvelle.

Loft
INTERNATIONAL **$$**

11 Map p106, B3

Carnivores unite. From Atlas mountain snails to lamb shank and a divine calf's liver (doused in a luscious garlicky sauce), Loft is a meat-lover's paradise. Framed by huge wall mirrors, the small space buzzes from lunch till late, but exceptionally on-the-ball staff keep service fast and friendly even when it's packed. (☑0524 43 42 16; 18 Rue de la Liberté; mains Dh130-190; ☉noon-midnight; ✷❄☎)

La Cuisine de Mona
LEBANESE **$$**

12 Map p106, A2

This tiny, colourful place is easily missed. Inside, it's all about Lebanese *mezze* (starter-style plates) with masses of choice for vegetarians. Feast on hummus, fattoush salad, *baba ghanoush* and *mujadara* (lentils

with caramelised onions) just like a Beiruti mama would make. Complete the picture with a bottle of wine from Lebanon's Bekaa Valley. (☑0618 13 79 59; 5 Residence Mamoune, 115B; mixed mezze platters Dh80-90, individual mezze Dh30-40; ☉10am-10.30pm Mon-Sat; ✷☑)

Chez Mado
SEAFOOD **$$**

13 Map p106, B3

With the fragrance of Oualidia's salty shallows still fresh on them, Chez Mado's oysters are the prettiest and plumpest in Marrakesh. Shellfish and seafood are delivered daily here, where under chef Alex Chaussetier's direction they are transformed into the lightest lunches: elegant sole meunière, grilled prawns and mayonnaise, John Dory with chorizo and a seafood platter to blow your mind. (☑0524 42 14 94; 22 Rue Moulay Ali; mains Dh90-220; ☉noon-3pm & 7-11.30pm Tue-Sun; ✷)

SALVADOR AZNAR/SHUTTERSTOCK ©

La Mamounia Hotel, home to the La Mamounia Gardens (p109)

Azar
MIDDLE EASTERN **$$$**

14 Map p106, B4

Imagine a Beirut lounge teleported to Marrakesh via Mars: with space-captain chairs and star-patterned stucco walls, the decor is out of this world and the Lebanese-inspired fare isn't far behind. The *mezze* is where this place really shines with pleasing *batata harra* and *chankliche*. Shared mixed *mezze* platters (from Dh190) will keep vegetarians happy and bills in this stratosphere. (📞0524 43 09 20; www.azarmarrakech.com; Rue de Yougoslavie; mains Dh95-250; ☉7pm-midnight; ✳🚭)

Local Life
Seafood Restaurants

The entire stretch of **Rue Maurltanie** is packed with sidewalk stalls and restaurants serving up seafood offerings. At weekend lunchtimes the pavement terraces are busy and buzzing with local families munching on fried fish.

Snack al-Bahriya (Map p106, B4; 75 Ave Moulay Rachid, cnr Rue Mauritanie; seafood with chips Dh30-80; ☉10am-midnight) is our pick of the bunch for dishing up fresh fish and perfectly tender fried calamari with generous chunks of lemon, plus salt, cumin and hot sauce.

L'Annexe

FRENCH $$

15 Map p106, B3

Head here for French lunches enjoyed in a mirrored cafe-bistro setting, handy to all the ville nouvelle boutique action. After you've eaten the umpteenth tajine, L'Annexe offers a welcome switch to light, clean flavours: it does Provençal fish soup, duck *confit* (duck slowly cooked in its own fat) atop salad and a mean crème brûlée. The three-course lunch menus (Dh120) are a winner. (☑0524 43 40 10; www.lannexemarrakech.com; 14 Rue Moulay Ali; mains Dh70-180; ☺noon-3pm & 7.30-11:30pm Mon-Sat; 🛜)

Drinking

68 Bar à Vin

BAR

16 Map p106, B3

A hip and ultra-lively little wine bar that packs in a nice mixed crowd of Moroccans and foreign residents. There are both European and Moroccan wines on offer as well as beer. Staff are on the ball and friendly. When it gets too smoky later in the evening, escape to the patio bench seating out the front. (☑0524 44 97 42; 68 Rue de la Liberté; ☺7pm-2am)

Grand Café de la Poste

CAFE

17 Map p106, C4

Restored to its flapper-era glory, this landmark bistro oozes colonial decadence in spades. Prices run high for dinner so skip the food and instead lap up the old-world ambience of dark wood and potted palms with a coffee, Darjeeling tea or wine in hand. (☑0524 43 30 38; cnr Blvd el-Mansour Eddahbi & Rue Imam Malik; ☺8am-1am; ❄🛜)

Pointbar

BAR

18 Map p106, B2

A lot of Marrakesh bars can get a bit smoky, which is why Pointbar with its outdoor front courtyard (which has a retractable roof for colder nights) is, literally, a breath of fresh air. Sit yourself down on a comfy sofa or square pouf, order from the tapas set menu (Dh210) and have a few beers. (3 Rue Abou Hayane Taouhidi; ☺6pm-late)

PICTUREPARTNERS/SHUTTERSTOCK ©

Flaky Moroccan pancakes with *bessara* (p111)

Kaowa
CAFE

19 Map p106, D2

Breezy Kaowa brings a touch of California cool to the Majorelle gardens. The decked terrace attracts a see-and-be-seen crowd who sip detox smoothies and lunch on huge slices of quiche and leafy salads (Dh75 to Dh90). (☑ 0524 33 00 72; 34 Rue Yves Saint Laurent; ☺ 8am-8pm; ❄ ☏)

L'auberge Espagnole
BAR

20 Map p106, B3

L'auberge Espagnole may not be able to decide if it's a restaurant, tapas bar, or sports bar, but heck, who cares? This friendly hang-out, with walls covered in sporting paraphernalia and big-screen TVs does a good line in Spanish tapas as well as imported and local beers. (Rue Moulay Ali; ☺ 5pm-1am)

Café du Livre
CAFE

21 Map p106, B3

This cafe-bar is a chilled-out spot with draft beer, cushy seating, walls of books to browse and quiz nights. Come for happy hour (6-8pm Tuesday to Saturday) for some of the cheapest beer in town (Dh20-40) when the after-work crowd descends and it takes on a lively pub atmosphere. (☑ 0524 43 21 49; www.cafedulivre.com; 44 Rue Tariq ibn Ziyad; ☺ 10am-11pm Mon-Sat; ❄ ☏)

 Top Tip

Moroccan Wine

Alcohol isn't widely served at medina restaurants, so head for the ville nouvelle if you want a drink. Moroccan wines are definitely worth a try. Look for these names when you're choosing your bottle:

White Try crisp, food-friendly Larroque; well-balanced, juicy Terre Blanche; and citrusy, off-dry Cuveé du Président Sémillant.

Gris and Rosé Look for not-too-fruity Medaillon Rosé de Syrah; fragrant Domain Rimal Vin Gris; and the crisply top-range Volubilia.

Red Reliable local red wines include the admirable burgundy-style Terre Rouge from Rabati coastal vineyards; well-rounded Volubilia from Morocco's ancient Roman wine-growing region; and the spicier merlot-syrah-cabernet sauvignon Coteaux Atlas.

Le Studio
BAR

22 Map p106, B4

This upmarket wine bar serves a sophisticated wine list and some impeccable French food. Sip smooth glasses of Domaine de Sahari while nibbling spiced olives at high tables, or dine beneath the open retractable roof, mopping up plates of lobster fricassee and beef fillet dusted with truffle shavings (Dh200 to Dh250). Suave hosts Steve and Didier circle the room lapping up compliments. (📞0524 43 37 00; 85 Ave Moulay Rachid; 📶)

Brasserie de Flore
CAFE

23 🚇 Map p106, C4

Most old ville nouvelle cafes have either been replaced or gutted and thoroughly modernised. But inside Brasserie de Flore a smidgeon of faded old-world ambience still clings on. Pop in for a coffee or a glass of wine to check out the curvy art nouveau mirrors. (Pl du 16 Novembre; ⏰10am-10pm; ❄️📶)

Djelabar
CLUB

24 🚇 Map p106, C5

Lounge-club-restaurant with a cabaret show on the weekends (cue the belly dancers) and plenty of over-the-top kitsch style. The converted stucco-tastic 1940s wedding hall features a bar with eye-popping *zellij* (ceramic tile mosaic) detail and wall portraits sporting fez-wearing icons from Marilyn Monroe to Michael Jackson. Skip the food; come for a late-night drink. (📞0524 42 12 42; 2 Rue Abou Hanifa, Hivernage; ⏰7pm-3am)

Entertainment

Comptoir
CLUB

25 ⭐ Map p106, D6

Looking for a venue that could out-bling a Kardashian? You got it. Join Casa playboys and glamour-puss Mar-rakshis to watch belly dancers strut their stuff before the DJs take over.

For the whole-hog spectacle come on Friday or Saturday when acrobats and cabaret performers in fancy dress mingle with the dance-floor crowd. (📞0524 43 77 02; www.comptoirdarna.com; Ave Echouhada; ⏰8pm-3am)

Le Colisée
CINEMA

26 ⭐ Map p106, B3

The plushest cinema in the central city, Le Colisée, near Rue Moham-med el-Beqal, has Dolby sound and a mixed-gender, Moroccan and foreign resident crowd. Films are sometimes in the original language (including English) and subtitled in French. (📞0524 44 88 93; Blvd Mohammed Zerk-touni; orchestra/balcony Dh25/35)

Shopping

33 Rue Majorelle
FASHION & ACCESSORIES

27 🔒 Map p106, D2

More than 60 designers, mostly from Morocco, are represented here and co-owner Yehia Abdelnour dedicates much of his time to sourcing local *maâlems* (master craftsmen) who make the majority of what's on view. Recent finds include super-cool clutches made in vintage upholstery from the Harakat sisters, silk harem pants from couturier Maroc n'Roll and plaited, pop-art charm bracelets from Zinab Chahine. (📞0524 31 41 95; www.33ruemajorelle.com; 33 Rue Yves Saint Laurent; ⏰9.30am-7pm)

A belly dancer performs at Comptoir

Ensemble Artisanal   ARTS & CRAFTS

28 Map p106, E5

To get a jump-start on the souqs, come to this government-sponsored showcase across from Cyber Park to glimpse expert artisans at work and see the range of crafts and prices Marrakesh has to offer. The set prices are higher than in the souqs, but it's hassle-free shopping and the producer gets paid directly. (Ave Mohammed V; ⏰9.30am-12.30pm & 3-7pm Mon-Sat)

Atika   SHOES

29 Map p106, B3

With more colours than a candy store, Atika loafers are a Marrakesh must-have. Some customers have been known to buy their favourite shoe in 10 different colours, and at Dh650 to Dh700 a pair, a quarter of the price of designer-brand lookalikes, who can blame them? (📞0524 43 95 76; 34 Rue de la Liberté; ⏰8.30am-12.30pm & 3.30-8pm Mon-Sat)

Darart Librairie   BOOKS

30 Map p106, D2

This bookshop sells glossy coffee-table books about Morocco, with a small selection of English as well as French titles. There's also a tiny shelf of Morocco travel guidebooks, good city and country maps, and a decent clutch of Moroccan cookery books. (📞0524 31 45 93; 79 Rue Yves Saint Laurent; ⏰9am-6pm)

L'Atelier du Vin   WINE

31 Map p106, A2

For Moroccan wines at realistic prices, head to this dedicated wine shop. (📞0524 45 71 12; 87 Rue Mohamed el-Beqal; ⏰9.30am-12.30pm & 3.30-8pm Mon-Sat)

Top Sights
Palmeraie

Getting There

🚗 **Taxi** Most visitors hire taxis for a return trip.

🚲 **Bicycle** The main Palmeraie Circuit road is accessed from both Rte de Casablanca and Rte de Fez.

If the tightly woven medina alleys are making you miss nature's open spaces, escape to the *palmeraie* (palm grove). Wrapped up in the legends of Marrakesh's beginnings, this sweep of greenery is now the haunt of hotels and chichi holiday homes. Plenty of resorts here offer afternoon lunch-and-pool deals, while quad-bike and dromedary rides offer a slice of desert fun.

Swimming at Nikki Beach in the *palmeraie*

Marrakesh's Green Lungs

According to legend, Marrakesh's *palmeraie* took root when the city's founding Berber army troops spat out their date stones here. Today this shady haven, edging Marrakesh's northwest corner, contains roughly 50,000 date palms which help keep temperatures lower than in the central city. The 5km 'Palmeraie Circuit' is speckled with villas and luxury resorts.

Modern Art & Garden Strolls

The **Musée de la Palmeraie** (☏0661 09 53 52; off Rte de Fez; adult/child Dh40/free; ☉9am-6pm) displays a so-so collection of modern art but is also home to two immaculate gardens (one with cacti, one Andalucian), which are a tranquil retreat. Along the same dusty track you'll find the **Musée Farid Belkahia** (☏0524 32 89 59; off Rte de Fez; adult/child Dh50/30; ☉10am-7pm), showcasing the work of Morocco's most famous contemporary artist.

Dromedary Rides

If you don't have time for a Sahara excursion, the *palmeraie* has dromedary stations at either end of the Palmeraie Circuit where you can experience a camel ride (about Dh50 to Dh70; bargain hard) between the palms. Rides last about 45 minutes and are tailored towards complete novice camel-riders. If that sounds too sedate and scenic, the dromedary stations also offer quad-bike (ATV) tours.

Saddling Up

For those who want to explore properly, **Les Cavaliers de L'Atlas** (☏0611 81 68 06; www.lescavaliers delatlas.com; Rte de Casablanca; half/full day €50/90) is a professional stable near the *palmeraie* offering half- and full-day rides through the *palmeraie* and into the Atlas countryside beyond. It has a mix of Arab, Anglo-Arab and Berber horses and can adapt rides for all ranges of riding experience and age.

Rte de Casablanca, 5km northwest of town

☑ Top Tip

▶ One of the best ways to explore the *palmeraie* is by bike. Cycling tours are offered by **AXS** (www. argansports.com; Rue Fatima al Fihria; half-day city tours from Dh350) and **Marrakech Bike Action** (www. marrakechbikeaction.com; 1st fl, 212 Ave Mohammed V; tours Dh250). They make for a family-friendly and gentle-paced country-side excursion from the central city.

✗ Take a Break

For a retreat treat, **Jnane Tamsna** (☏0524 32 94 23; www.jnane.com; Douar Abiad; ❄☎☀) offers lunch-and-pool deals for Dh400 per person within its 3.5-hectare property of lush land scaped gardens.

The huge pool at **Palais Mehdi** (☏0524 30 75 77; www.palais-mehdi.com; Circuit de la Palmeraie) makes for a relaxing afternoon. Pool access for lunch diners is Dh200 per person.

The Best of
Marrakesh

Interior decoration, Dar Si Said (p86)
DAVE STAMBOULIS/AGE FOTOSTOCK ©

Best Walks
Monumental Medina

🏃 The Walk

Take a stroll down a Marrakesh memory lane and hit all of the city's major historic monuments in one swoop. These are the grand palaces and religious buildings – hidden behind high nondescript walls – that Marrakesh's sultans and pashas bequeathed to the pink-walled city to raise it into their imperial capital.

Start Ali ben Youssef Medersa

Finish Saadian Tombs

Length 4km; three hours

🍴 Take a Break

Marrakesh's main square **Djemaa el-Fna** (p24) is rimmed by cafes and restaurants where you can grab a bite or just a drink. Try **Café Kessabine** (p33) to munch on *pastilla* (rich savoury-sweet pie) or simply grab an orange juice from one of the square's juice stands.

Decorative detail, Ali ben Youssef Medersa

PHILIP REEVE/SHUTTERSTOCK ©

❶ Ali ben Youssef Medersa

Step inside the Ali ben Youssef Medersa (p60) and find yourself surrounded by contemplative beauty that soothes away the distractions of the outside world. The joyful flurry of *zellij* (ceramic tile mosaic) and intricate carved wood here, though, must have provided ample distraction to students trying to study within this old religious seminary.

❷ Musée de Marrakech

The Mnebhi Palace once was the stage for the highfalutin lifestyles of Marrakesh's rich and powerful, but now plays host to the Musée de Marrakech (p62), displaying both modern and ancient art exhibits.

❸ Koutoubia Mosque

No other monument is so symbolic of Marrakesh. With its mathematically pleasing proportions, bestowed by Almohad architects, the golden-hued stone minaret of the Koutoubia Mosque (p26) is the city's most recognisable sight.

4 Dar Si Said

A rich riot of *zouak* (painted wood) work graces the ceilings of the 1st-floor salons in the Dar Si Said (p86), which is also home to the exhibits of the Museum of Moroccan Arts.

5 Bahia Palace

It's not called La Bahia (the beautiful) for nothing. Bahia Palace (p82) is a triumphant vision of opulence created by Grand Vizier Si Moussa on a 14-year interior decoration binge. The work on the cedar-wood ceilings is a masterful display of what can be achieved when Moroccan *mâalems* (master artisans) are firing on all cylinders.

6 Mellah

Take a break from bygone glitz and immerse yourself in Marrakesh's *mellah*, where the city's Jewish community once lived. As well as dipping into the tangle of alleyways, you can visit the Lazama Synagogue (p90) and the white tombs of the Miaâra (p90; Jewish cemetery).

7 Badi Palace

The once mighty 16th-century Badi Palace (p89) – El-Badi (the incomparable) – now lies in jagged ruins, having been destroyed less than 100 years after al-Mansour ordered that it be built.

8 Saadian Tombs

The Saadian Tombs (p84), where al-Mansour lies in rest, are an extravagance of marble and ornate plasterwork that showcase the Saadian era's flair for interior overkill.

Best Walks
Souq Strolling

The Walk

Marrakesh is defined by its dawdling lanes of souqs, which bend and turn in what seems an unfathomable maze. This is the very core of this historic trading post, where caravans emerged from their long journeys to buy, sell and trade. Today although travellers arrive by plane and train, not camel, Marrakesh's long tradition of commerce and artisan work continues. Explore the bustling market streets, artisan quarters and pink-hued muddling alleys that make up the medina's centre.

Start Djemaa el-Fna

Finish Place Rahba Kedima

Length 2km; two hours

Take a Break

In Mouassine both Kafe Fnaque Berbère (p32) and Dar Cherifa (p52) are welcoming places for a pot of tea and a snack while you consult your map to prepare for further souq exploits.

❶ Djemaa el-Fna

The best place to get your bearings for a souq assault is Djemaa el-Fna (p24). Marrakesh's main square is the pumping heart of the medina, with arteries of souqs threading out in all directions. The main entertainment here doesn't start thumping until dusk, but even during the day this place is a hive of energy.

❷ Rue Mouassine

Head north through Souq Ablueh (the olive souq) and turn west onto Souq Quessabine until you hit the small square of Place Bab Fteuh. From here it's a straight (well, as straight as a souq can be) stroll north on Rue Mouassine. Stores along this lane sell jewellery, ceramics and *babouches* (leather slippers).

❸ Musée de Mouassine

The alley that leads behind the Mouassine Mosque is a narrow squiggle of pink. Follow it to Musée de Mouassine (p45) to view the jewel-coloured interior that has been painstak-

CHRIS HEPBURN/GETTY IMAGES ©
Colourful tajines for sale

ingly restored to its former glory.

④ Souq des Teinturiers

Meander your way back to the mosque and dive head first into the souq streets to the north. Souq des Teinturiers (p46) is the dyer's souq. Check out the rainbow-haul of wool skeins swinging from the rafters and the pots of dye-powder sitting beside the cubby-hole workshops.

⑤ Souq Haddadine

Souq Kchachbia is a mainline for souvenir shopping, but if you can pull yourself away from all that glitters and veer east you'll hit Souq Haddadine (p67; Blacksmith's Souq). The shops here are full of artisans at work and a good opportunity to buy direct from the producer.

⑥ The Qissariat

Head onto Souq Smata and then get ready to lose your bearings slightly as you weave into the *qissariat* (covered markets). This warren of passages lies in the centre of the souq area and still holds onto

its traditional feel. This is a good place to bargain for *babouches*.

⑦ Place Rahba Kedima

The *qissariat* alleys all join onto Souq el-Kebir, from where it's only a

short hop to Place Rahba Kedima. Hawkers on the central square sell handmade souvenirs while spice fans will appreciate the heady scents of cumin and cinnamon surrounding the apothecary stores here.

Best
Food

Marrakesh's culinary scene has improved considerably with a flurry of new restaurants opening in both the medina and ville nouvelle. That said, as traditionally Marrakshis don't eat out often, most medina restaurants are aimed squarely at the tourist market and meals can be hit-and-miss. In middle-class Guéliz, there's more of a local dining vibe with both Moroccan and international restaurants.

Riad Dadas

The *dadas* (chefs) who work in the medina's riads are the unsung heroes of Marrakesh's culinary scene. Many riads open up their courtyard or rooftop restaurant to nonguests so you can sample different *dadas'* takes on Moroccan specialities. In nearly all cases, you have to book ahead due to both limited seating and so the *dadas* can plan the menu in advance.

Snak Attack

The street-food scene is thriving in Marrakesh, so don't be afraid to jump on in. Hard-working souq workers with no time for a long lazy lunch head to a *snak* (kiosk) to feast on peppery *merguez* (spicy lamb sausage), *teyhan* (stuffed spleen) and *brochettes* (kebabs). Join the queue at the one thronged with locals for the freshest, tastiest food.

Fusion Fad

French cuisine has always played a role in Marrakesh's modern culinary scene, but recently more restaurants are playing around with Middle Eastern, Italian and Spanish cooking traditions and merging them with Moroccan flavours. This Mediterranean fusion style can be a tasty break when you've eaten your fill of tajines.

☑ **Top Tips**

▶ Many restaurants offer *prix fixe* (fixed price) three-course lunch menus which are similar to but much better value than a dinner menu; great for budget-conscious gourmets.

▶ Advance reservations are recommended (and sometimes essential) for most top-end restaurants.

▶ Alcohol is not widely available in medina restaurants.

▶ Top-end restaurants usually open between noon and 2.30pm, and 7.30pm and 11pm.

Moroccan tajine dishes

Just Like Mamma's

Amal Center Top lunch-time feasting on Moroccan home cooking, plus you support a worthy cause. (p109)

Naima Family-run restaurant that serves up superior couscous made fresh daily. (p71)

Traditional Feasts

Al Fassia Hands-down the best *mezze* (starter-size plates) in Marrakesh. (p110)

Le Tobsil Bring a hearty appetite for the Moroccan five-course dinner extravaganza here. (p30)

Riads & Rooftops

La Maison Arabe The regal surroundings makes for a dinner with serious style cred. (p50)

PepeNero Charming service and courtyard dining beside the pool with both classic Italian and Moroccan menus. (p92)

Dar Anika The rooftop may be bijou but the flavours are bold. (p91)

Modern Moroccan-Mediterranean

Gastro MK Book as far in advance as possible to experience this riad's innovative Moroccan-Mediterranean menu. (p31)

Latitude 31 Traditional dishes get a makeover with contemporary tweaks and a slice of fusion flair. (p51)

Eating Like a Local

Hadj Mustapha The best place in town to dig into Marrakshi crockpot speciality *tanjia*. (p31)

Snack al-Bahriya Fish and chips the Moroccan way. (p113)

Mechoui Alley Slow-roasted lamb straight from the pit oven. Enough said. (p31)

Sweet Treats

Pâtisserie Amandine The macarons here give hot-shot Parisian patisseries a run for their money. (p110)

Panna Gelato When the going gets hot, head here for Italian gelato with Moroccan flavours. (p109)

Best Shopping

Think of the medina's souqs as a shopping mall, but laid out according to a labyrinthine medieval-era plan. Whether you want to spice up your pantry with North African flavours or buy a carpet to add Moroccan-wow to your house, this magpie's nest of treasures is manna for shop-til-you-drop fanatics.

MICHAEL HEFFERNAN/LONELY PLANET ©

Souq Know-How

'Souq' means 'market', but when locals refer to 'the souqs' they mean the maze of market streets north of the Djemaa el-Fna and southwest of the Musée de Marrakesh. The main thoroughfare from the Djemaa el-Fna, **Souq Semmarine** (Leather Souq), sells a hodgepodge of local crafts. Prices are at their most expensive here, given the high price of real estate on the main drag, and products often come from specialist souqs just a few streets away. It is always better to buy products direct in dedicated souqs, especially in the case of carpets, metalware and leatherwork. The smaller *qissariat* (covered markets), which run between **Souqs Smata** and **el-Kebir** (literally, 'the big souq'), usually have lower-priced crafts.

Carpets

Creiee Berbere is the carpet souq but you'll find carpet shops scattered throughout the city. Whatever you're dreaming could look great in your lounge, know your limits: namely, how much floorspace you actually have. Tread cautiously with claims of antique carpets. New rugs are sometimes 'aged' by being stomped on or bleached by the sun. Also, understand what factors boost carpet value. Natural dyes and a higher number of knots per sq cm cost more. For more on carpet buying, see p77.

Cooperative Shopping

Al Kawtar Fabulous hand-stitched household linens made by a collective of women with disabilities. (p55)

Assouss Cooperative d'Argane Gorgeous argan essential oils to slather over skin, sold by a women's cooperative. (p55)

Al Nour Buy delicately embroidered cotton clothes and support this cooperative run by artisans with disabilities. (p37)

Art & Crafts

Anamil A high-quality haul of ceramics, textiles and leatherware for those hunting for something special. (p74)

Carpets on display at a souq stall

Maison de la Photographie Take a bit of history home with you from the vintage photography selection here. (p64)

Dar Chrifa Lamrania Modern art Moroccan-style (p74)

Fondouq el Ouarzazi A magpie-hoard of traditional Berber and Tuareg crafts. (p37)

Modern Moroccan Design

Souk Cherifa Young designers pitch their claim on the upper-balcony salons selling quirky accessories and homewares. (p55)

33 Rue Majorelle Expert craftspeople create contemporary twists on ancient design. (p116)

Chabi Chic Traditional tajines and tea-glasses get a modern makeover. (p74)

Moroccan Fashion & Beauty

Naturom Heavenly potions and lotions all fully organic and locally made. (p97)

Max & Jan Medina fashion goes full-hipster. (p56)

Norya Ayron Floaty designer dresses worn by Hollywood A-listers (p56)

Worth a Trip

The industrial quarter of **Sidi Ghanem** (www. sidighanem.net; Rte de Safi; ⊙9am-6pm Mon-Fri, 9am-noon Sat) is located 4km outside the centre of Marrakesh. It is chock-full of design studios selling direct from their outlets. This is where to pick up modern spins on Moroccan ceramics and textiles as well as enough traditional artisan crafts and furniture to kit out your own riad.

Best
Arts & Crafts

Palaces are a riot of tilework detail, floral designs and swirling carved decoration, and riads are decked out with intricate plasterwork. Marrakesh is a city steeped in ancient artistry and those traditions are kept alive by the modern craftspeople of the souqs and contemporary art scene of the ville nouvelle.

Traditional Techniques

Brush up on craft know-how before you view Marrakesh's monuments or trawl the souqs for a slice of Moroccan artistry. *Zellij* is a mosaic of glazed tiles fitted into intricate geometric designs while *zouak* is a painted-wood technique used to high effect on door panels and cedar-wood ceilings.

In the souqs you'll see ceramic crafts from across Morocco, but you can stick to local goods: Marrakesh specialises in monochrome ceramics in red, graphite and orange. For traditional textile techniques, look out for blue-and-white patterned *terz fezzi* linens and colourful silk Rabati embroidery. And keep your eyes peeled for *passementerie* (trims) *mâalems* (master artisans) at work, hand-spinning thread from a nail stuck in the souq wall to create silken tassels and knotted buttons.

Contemporary Art

Trailblazing Marrakesh is the centre of Morocco's small but growing modern-art scene. Marrakesh's contemporary artists combine elemental forms with organic, traditional materials, merging abstract with indigenous art forms. The scene has taken off in the past decade with the Marrakech Biennale (www.marrakechbiennale.com) launched in 2005, and the ville nouvelle is now home to several art galleries.

SELEZNYOV OLEG/SHUTTERSTOCK ©

☑ **Top Tip**

▶ Moroccan ceramics are excellent value – a decorative tajine may cost you Dh150 to Dh400, depending on size and decoration, making this a great piece of local craft work to take home. Be aware, though, that most decorative tajines are not oven-safe and are for ornamental use only.

Elaborate *zouak* painted ceiling, Bahia Palace (p82)

Craftspeople at Work

Ensemble Artisanal
Head here for a gander at local craftspeople and artisans at work (p117)

Souq Haddadine
The medina's blacksmiths have their workshops here. (p67)

Galleries

MACMA
Artworks from the big names of Orientalist art. (p108)

Musée Farid Belkahia
Well-curated selection of works from one of Morocco's most lauded 20th-century artists. (p119)

Galerie Rê
The city's funkiest contemporary art space. (p105)

Dar Bellarj
Old stork hospital converted into a gallery devoted to promoting local art heritage. (p69; pictured above left)

Artisan Interiors

Ali ben Youssef Medersa
The artistry of Islamic architecture reaches its peak in the courtyard of this theological college. (p60)

Bahia Palace
It ain't called 'The Beautiful' for nothing, you know. (p82)

Saadian Tombs
An interior that was worth dying for. (p84)

Musée de Mouassine
A jewel box of domestic interior design restored to its Saadian-era glory. (p45)

Musée de Marrakech
The lavish central courtyard is a showcase of swirling stucco, carved wood and *zellij*. (p62)

Unusual Crafts

Creations Pneumatiques
Collect your sustainable-art brownie points here with recycled tyre-tread crafts. (p98)

Best
Berber Culture

ANDRZEJ KUBIK/SHUTTERSTOCK ©

Marrakesh has Amazigh (Berber) roots, founded by the tribes of the Atlas Mountains who became the Almoravid dynasty. Through its long history this city has kept up its Berber connection, functioning over the centuries as a vital commercial hub where Amazigh tribes came to buy and sell. These associations remain strong and Berber culture is alive and well in Marrakesh.

Berber Folk Music

To experience a slice of Berber culture while you're in Marrakesh, catch a Berber folk-music performance. Berber music uses a minimum of accompanying instruments, usually depending on a drum to set the rhythm and the flute to carry the tune. Because of the huge diversity of different Amazigh tribes, there is a rich breadth of musical styles under the Berber umbrella.

The Marrakech Festival of Popular Arts (p134) is a great time to be in the city if you want to catch a variety of Berber folk-music groups. At other times, head to Djemaa el-Fna in the evening. On any given night the square plays host to some Berber musicians.

Musée Berbère Don't miss this stunning collection of Berber artefacts, art, textiles and jewellery at Jardin Majorelle. (p103)

Maison Tiskiwin Berber artefacts and craftwork take prime position in anthropologist Bert Flint's collection of indigenous crafts. (p89)

Cafe Clock Every Saturday night from 6pm, this cafe in the kasbah area hosts Berber musicians. (p91)

Dar Si Said Leatherware and textiles of the Berber peoples make up part of the museum collection here. (p86)

Djemaa el-Fna Among the soothsayers and snake charmers, you'll find Berber bands entertaining the crowds in the evenings. (p24)

Musée Boucharouite Berber rag-rugs take centre stage at this popular arts museum highlighting lesser-known crafts. (p69)

Heritage Museum Berber costumes and textiles make up some of the exhibits at this excellent small museum. (p29)

Best
Faith & Traditions

LENAR MUSIN/SHUTTERSTOCK ©

You'll understand how religion permeates the rhythms of daily life when you hear the sonorous call to prayer echo out from the mosques. As an old imperial capital, Marrakesh is home to some beautiful examples of Islamic religious architecture, but it also holds on to a heritage of other religious communities who once made this city a vibrant caravan town.

☑ Top Tips

▶ Wear clothing that covers shoulders and knees while in the medina, to respect older, and more traditional, Moroccans.

▶ If greeted with es salaam alaykum (peace be upon you), reply with wa alaykum salaam (and upon you be peace).

▶ Non-Muslims cannot enter any of Marrakesh's mosques or religious shrines.

Things to Remember

If this is your first visit to a Muslim country you may wonder how this will affect your trip. The main point is, it won't. Sunday is the official day off for shops and banks, and on Fridays (the Muslim holy day) most souq shops close, particularly in the traditional workshop areas. Alcohol is freely available in restaurants, bars and bigger supermarkets in the ville nouvelle, although due to expensive alcohol licenses it is harder to source in the medina. If travelling during Ramadan (the Muslim holy month of fasting) you're not expected fast but should refrain from eating and smoking in public during daylight.

Koutoubia Mosque The golden stone Koutoubia Minaret is the landmark of the city. (p26)

Miaâra Tranquil, sprawling Jewish cemetery on the edge of the atmospheric cramped alleyways of the mellah (Jewish quarter). (p90)

Ali ben Youssef Medersa This religious seminary is one of Mo-

rocco's best examples of Islamic artistry. (p60)

Zawiya Sidi Bel-Abbes Marrakesh's most important marabout zawiya (shrine honouring a saint). (p79)

Lazama Synagogue Still-functioning synagogue also with exhibits documenting Morocco's Jewish community. (p90)

Koutoubia Minbar Spectacular prayer pulpit now residing in Badi Palace. (p89)

Best
Festivals

MICHAEL HEFFERNAN/LONELY PLANET ©

Marrakesh hosts an annual program of festivals befitting its self-proclaimed role as Morocco's cultural capital. From contemporary art and film to traditional song and dance, Marrakesh loves to get its glad rags on and play host. Tickets to events can generally be bought beforehand through festival websites or at official ticket outlets in town.

Marrakech Festival of Popular Arts (🕙Jul) The only thing hotter than Marrakesh in July is this free-form folk fest. Berber musicians, dancers and street performers from around the country pour into Marrakesh to thrill the masses.

Marrakech Biennale (www.marrakechbien nale.org; 🕙Feb-May) Promoting debate and dialogue through artistic exchange, this major trilingual (Arabic, French and English) festival invites local and international artists to create literary, artistic, architectural and digital works throughout the city. Held every other year (even years).

Marrakesh International Film Festival (www.festivalmarrakech.info/en/; 🕙Dec) Stars from Hollywood to Bollywood strut the Berber red carpet at this week-long festival, culminating in wildly unpredictable awards shows. There are also movie screenings at Djemaa el-Fna.

Marrakesh Marathon (www.marathon-marrakech. com; half-/full-marathon fee €50/70; 🕙Jan) Run like there's a carpet salesperson after you, from the Djemaa to the *palmeraie* and back, for this annual marathon.

Oasis Festival (www.oasis fest.com; 🕙Sep) Brings together Morocco's best electronica talent with DJs from Europe for a music festival with a distinctly Moroccan twist. In the afternoon there's swimming, a souq, yoga and henna art; once dusk sets in the DJs hit the decks.

TEDx Marrakesh (www. tedxmarrakesh.net; adult/student €98/25; 🕙Oct) Like any self-respecting cultural capital, Marrakesh has its own TEDx talkfest, where Marrakshi movers and shakers take on challenging themes such as 'Driving Forces' and 'Coexistence or No Existence'.

MadJazz (www.madjazz-festival.com; 🕙May) Marrakesh invents new sounds nightly with Gnaoua castanets, jazz riffs and Jimi Hendrix guitar licks.

Best
With Kids

The mutual admiration between kids and Marrakesh is obvious. Kids will gaze in wonderment at fairy-tale souq scenes and the chaotic, thrumming spectacle of Djemaa el-Fna lit up at night. That said, for families with toddlers and babies the city can be overwhelming and logistically challenging. Careful planning takes the stress out of visiting Marrakesh with younger children.

Riad Plusses & Minuses

The key to a successful trip is child-friendly accommodation. Fair warning: riad plunge pools and steep stairs aren't exactly childproof, and sound reverberates through riad courtyards. Most riad owners and staff, however, dote on babies and will provide cots and high chairs, and cater special meals on request.

No-Cost Entertainment

Marrakesh museums are a poor substitute for the live theatre of the souqs and the Djemaa el-Fna. Mornings are quieter in the souqs, meaning less hassle and a better view of craftspeople at work. Early evenings (6pm to 8pm) are best for Djemaa dance troupes and musicians, and offer chance encounters with Moroccan families also doing the rounds.

Beldi Country Club

(☏0524 38 39 50; www.beldicountryclub.com; Rte de Barrage 'Cherifa', Km6; adult/child pool day-pass Dh200/100, incl lunch Dh370/250; ☙) A 15-hectare country retreat designed with families in mind; includes a children's pool and child-focused activities ranging from bread baking to horse riding.

Terres d'Amanar

(☏0524 43 81 03; www.terresdamanar.com; Douar Akli, Tahanaoute; activities from Dh100; ☙) Adrenaline-packed activities to balance out all that souq strolling. This outdoor centre, 36km south of Marrakesh, offers zip lines, a forest adventure course, mountain biking and horse riding.

Oasiria

(☏0524 38 04 38; www.oasiria.com; Rte d'Amizmiz, Km4; adult/child Dh210/130; ☙10am-6pm; ☙) Beat the heat with nine pools, a kamikaze slide and a pirate lagoon, all tucked within lush gardens.

Creative Interactions

(☏0524 42 16 87; www.creative-interactions.com; Apt 47, Imm. El Khalil Bldg, Ave des Nations Unies; private/group 1½hr €40/35, 3hr €65/60) Family-friendly activities such as a task-filled medina hunt and henna-art workshops.

Best
Spas & Hammams

The quintessential Moroccan experience: after a day of dusty sightseeing exploits, a good scrubbing leaves you squeaky clean, fresh and invigorated. Public hammams are not for the faint of heart but are great for local interaction. The city's flourishing private hammam scene allows the less adventurous a more refined and relaxing experience.

Bathing Rituals

A hammam at its simplest is a steam bath where you wash yourself down, sweat out the dirt of the day and then scrub, with an optional massage afterwards. For many Moroccans hammams are as much a social occasion (particularly for women) as they are about bathing. If you're going to go local with a public hammam be aware that a few don't accept non-Muslims. It's best to ask for hammam recommendations from locals.

Hammam History

Public baths were first introduced to Morocco and the rest of North Africa by the Romans. After Islam gained a foothold across the region, the baths were adapted to fit in with Islamic ablution rituals – foregoing the communal Roman bathing pool to use running water to wash under instead.

What Happens, Where

Hammams are made up of three interconnected areas: the *caldarium* (hot room), the *tepidarium* (warm room) and the *frigidarium* (cool room).

You sweat the dirt out and *gommage* (scrub) in the steamy hot room, sluice yourself down with buckets of water in the warm room, and relax afterwards in the cool room. For etiquette, see p49.

☑ **Top Tips**

▶ Public hammams are usually open for women during the day and men during the evening, though there are some exceptions to the rule.

▶ It's best to book ahead for private hammams.

▶ Many private hammams offer package deals for couples.

Public Hammams

Hammam Mouassine
The best choice for newbies, with professional staff used to travellers and bath-and-scrub packages offered. (p46)

Hammam Dar el-Bacha
Head here for a fully local hammam experience. (p50)

ITALIANVIDEOPHOTOAGENCY/SHUTTERSTOCK ©

Bathing at a traditional hammam

Hammam Bab Douk-kala Historic public hammam dating from the 17th century. Good local choice for male travellers. (p50)

Midrange Private Hammams

Hammam de la Rose Friendly staff, relaxed ambience and a host of add-on beauty and massage options. (p48)

Medina Spa Staff here are known for their great massages. (p30)

Hammam Ziani Less spruced-up than others, but superfriendly mas-seuses make it a good choice for females. (p90)

Private Hammam-Spas

Le Bain Bleu Stylish surroundings and luxurious spa-like services. Go on, treat yourself. (p47)

Heritage Spa A bevy of rejuvenating deep-cleansing treatments are on offer at this swish spa. (p47)

Sultana Spa Opulent marble-clad interiors and numerous pampering treatments and massage packages. (p90)

Worth a Trip
The rustic adobe-walled retreat of **Ferme Berbère**, 9km south of the city centre, offers excellent-value packages including hammam, lunch and pool access with special deals for families. It's a perfect escape from the medina hustle.

Best
Bars & Nightlife

Marrakesh doesn't have a huge nightlife scene, but in recent years there's been a (small) flurry of trendy bar openings in Guéliz in the ville nouvelle. Saturday night is the best night for clubbing fans – other days tend to be much quieter.

Drinking in the Medina

The medina only has a handful of restaurants and bars licensed to serve alcohol, although many riads sell beer and wine to guests in the privacy of their inner courtyards. Restaurants that serve alcohol are generally happy for you to come in just for a drink.

68 Bar à Vin This tiny wine bar manages to squeeze in a fun and lively crowd. (p114)

Kechmara Ultra-hip bar-restaurant with an arty vibe and good music. (p105)

Pointbar The chilled-out front garden terrace here is a favourite with young Moroccans. (p114)

Café Arabe Head here for cocktails as the sun sets over the medina. (p52)

Kosybar Relax with a beer while watching the storks preen themselves on Badi Palace's ancient ramparts. (p95)

Grand Café de la Poste Bar-bistro with oodles of old-world ambience. (p114)

Café du Livre Cafe-bar with draught beer, board games, quiz nights and strong cocktails. (p115)

Piano Bar Refined surroundings and a jazz soundtrack for a quiet drink to top off the day. (p34)

Djelabar Pop-art interiors and a belly-dancing cabaret show. (p116)

☑ Top Tips

▸ Most clubs charge entry fees ranging from Dh150 to Dh350, including the first drink, but midweek those who arrive early and dress smartly may get in free.

▸ You have to be a night-owl to sample Marrakesh's club scene. Most clubs don't kick off until after midnight.

Comptoir The Marrakshi version of bling with a cabaret extravaganza thrown in for good measure. (p116; pictured above)

LONELY PLANET/GETTY IMAGES ©

Best
Sports &
Activities

AXS (🕿 0524 40 02 07; www.argansports.com; Rue Fatima al Fihria; half-day city tours from Dh350; 👬) Get on a bike and discover Marrakesh's sights on a classic city ride, or munch through street stalls between rides on the tasting tour. Those up for more adventure can mountain-bike in the Atlas or cycle to Essaouira. High-quality Giant road bikes, mountain bikes (including kid's bikes) and helmets provided.

Riad Bledna (🕿 0661 18 20 90; www.riadbledna. com; off Rte de Ouarzazate, Km19, 31°35'46.8"N 7°52'28.5"W; per person, incl lunch & transfer €25) This 1.5-hectare organic garden retreat is in a quiet Marrakesh suburb east of the city centre. Day rates offer superb value, covering use of the oxygen-filtered pool, tasty homemade lunches and transfers to and from Djemaa el-Fna.

Marrakech Bike Action (🕿 0661 24 01 45; www.mar rakechbikeaction.com; 1st fl, 212 Ave Mohammed V; city or palmeraie tour Dh250) Organises city and *palmeraie* tour circuits as well as mountain-biking day trips and longer excursions into the Atlas region. It also has electric-assisted mountain bikes for travellers worried about their ability to keep up with the rest of the group.

Morocco Adventure & Rafting (🕿 0661 77 52 51; www.rafting.ma; Rue Beni Marine; half-day rafting trip €95; 🕙 rafting available Feb–May) This local company has been leading rafting expeditions in the Atlas for over 12 years, with a team of local and international guides all with a minimum of five years' guiding experience. Excursions range from a half-day whitewater-rafting trip to Ourika to a three-day or week-long rafting excursion in the Ahansel Valley.

Beldi Country Club (🕿 0524 38 39 50; www. beldicountryclub.com; Rte de Barrage 'Cherifa', Km6; adult/child pool day pass Dh200/100, incl lunch Dh370/250; 👬) Located just 6km south of the city centre, the Beldi feels a million miles away from the dust and chaos of the medina. Lie back and smell the 15,000 roses at Dominique Leymarie's eco-chic paradise with its pools, spa, hammam, tennis courts and plenty of family-friendly activities on offer.

Best
Courses & Tours

Souk Cuisine (📞0673 80 49 55; www.soukcuisine. com; Zniquat Rahba, 5 Derb Tahtah; class incl meal & wine €50) Learn to cook as the *dadas* (chefs) do: shop in the souq for ingredients with English-speaking Dutch hostess Gemma van de Burgt, work alongside two Moroccan *dadas*, then enjoy the four-course lunch you helped cook. Courses are two-person minimum, 12 participants maximum; vegetarian courses possible.

Ateliers d'Ailleurs (📞0672 81 20 46; www.atel iersdailleurs.com; workshops €35-69) Engaging a select network of professional craftsmen with robust businesses in pottery, *tadelakt* (limestone plastering), woodwork, *zellij* tiling, embroidery and much more, these ateliers (studios) offer a unique insight into traditional craft techniques. During the two- to five-hour workshops, you work alongside craftspeople utilising traditional materials, with

enough time to practise several techniques and create your own objects.

Tawada Trekking (📞0618 24 44 31; www. tawadatrekking.com; Hay Ezzaitoun) Trekking tours into the Atlas Mountains, rafting trips and cultural immersion experiences are the speciality of this small, professional company run by Hafida H'doubane, one of the first Moroccan women to be licensed as a mountain guide.

Marrakech Food Tours (www.marrakechfoodtours. com; US$65; ⏰1pm & 6pm Sat-Thu) Munch your way through the medina: weave through the souqs tucking into *tanjia*, sampling Marrakshi street food and slurping down avocado milkshakes. Hosts Youssef and Amanda take groups (up to six participants) on a whirlwind tour of Marrakshi flavours. Bring your appetite.

Inside Morocco Travel (📞0524 43 00 20; www. insidemoroccotravel.com;

TONY ZELENOFF/SHUTTERSTOCK ©

4th fl, 29 Rue de Yougosla-vie; ⏰8.30am-4.30pm) Bespoke adventures designed by multilingual Mohamed Nour and his team. They specialise in High Atlas trekking trips and combined desert and mountain 4x4 excursions. Their day trip visiting the Agafay Desert, Lalla Takerkoust and hiking around Imlil (from €60 per person) is worthwhile if you're short of time.

Creative Interactions (📞0524 42 16 87; www. creative-interactions.com; Apt 47, Imm. El Khalil Bldg, Ave des Nations Unies; private/group 1½hr €40/35, 3hr €65/60) Fun and friendly Moroccan Arabic classes designed for short-term travellers. Learn the basics you'll most need on your visit.

Best
Gardens

KAJZRPHOTOGRAPHY/SHUTTERSTOCK ©

Outside of the medina's dense confines, Marrakesh is a surprisingly green city of vast gardens, many of which were once the exclusive domain of royalty. Many of the parks are fine relaxing territory so join the Marrakshis who come here to picnic, take an early-evening stroll or just beat the heat within their shady confines.

Royal Parks

Marrakesh's largest parks are the Menara Gardens, southwest of the ville nouvelle, and the Agdal Gardens, southeast of the kasbah. Note that the entries to both are a good half hour walk (45 minutes to Agdal) from Djemaa el-Fna and, although vast, most of the space is taken up with scrubby olive groves. Nevertheless, both boast reflective pools which provide each park's focal point and are a popular hang-out spot for local families and courting couples on the weekend. In summary, unless you're really into olive groves, the more central gardens are a much better bet if you're looking for a spot of chill-out time from the medina.

CyberPark Take a break between the medina and the ville nouvelle in this tranquil, well-manicured garden. (p108)

La Mamounia Gardens The historic hotel garden where Churchill once relaxed with his paintbrushes. (p109)

Jardin Majorelle Beautiful garden (pictured above) once owned by Yves Saint Laurent and home to the excellent Musée Berbère. (p102)

Le Jardin Secret A traditional medina garden reinvented for the 21st century. (p45)

Koutoubia Gardens A welcome, shady spot near Djemaa el-Fna with palm trees and manicured flower beds. (p29)

Musée de la Palmeraie Peaceful cacti and Andalucian gardens stretch behind this art gallery in the *palmeraie*. (p119)

Best
Countryside
Escapes

The moon-like expanse of the Agafay Desert is 40km southwest of Marrakesh while High Atlas town Ouirgane is only another 20km away. Both are playgrounds for weekending Marrakshis who come to dose up on fresh air and nature. Take a time-out from city life with an overnight trip to catch a glimpse of Morocco's rawly beautiful natural scenery.

OLIVER HOFFMANN/SHUTTERSTOCK ©

La Pause (☎0661 30 64 94; www.lapause-marrakech.com; Douar Lmih Laroussiéne, N 31°26.57, W 008°10.31; d per person incl full board in safari tent/lodge €135/200; ☲) Skip off the grid to this Agafay Desert getaway. This is a relaxation zone for grown-ups where electricity and smartphone checking is out, hammock swinging and nomad-tent dining is in, and you bed down in rustic-chic bungalows complete with candles, *tataoui* ceilings and Berber carpets.

L'Oliveraie de Marigha (☎0524 48 42 81; www.oliveraie-de-marigha.com; Km 59 R203, Douar Marigha; d/ste Dh900/1300; ⓟ❄🔉☲) Weekend escapees come all the way from Casa to rest in this olive grove and float in the pool admiring High Atlas views. Chic bungalows in subtle earth tones sit amid the trees and are equipped with walnut furniture, double-glazed French doors and shiny marble bathrooms.

Scarabeo (☎0662 80 08 23; www.scarabeo-camp.com; d/ste/f incl half-board Dh2055/2755/3080; ⊗closed mid-Jun–mid-Sep) Tuareg nomads never saw camping like this. Scarabeo's white nomad-style tents, complete with carpets and comfy beds, are set in the barren Agafay desert with panoramic views stretching to the Atlas Mountains. During the day spend your time trekking, riding camels, or exploring by 4x4; at night simply look up for unforgettable stargazing.

Ouirgane Ecolodge (☎0668 76 01 65; www.ouirgane-ecolodge.com; r Dh400-800; ❄🔉☲) For a peaceful escape from busy Marrakesh, it's hard to fault this environmentally minded retreat. Rooms boast a warm Berber design, and the lounge is a fine place for a meal or to curl up by the fireside with a good book. You can also use the hammam, lounge by the pool, hire mountain bikes or take scenic walks in the surrounding countryside.

Survival Guide

Survival Guide

Before You Go

When to Go

°C/°F **Temp**
40/104 —
30/86 —
20/68 —
10/50 —
0/32 —

Rainfall inches/mm
— 8/200
— 6/150
— 4/100
— 2/50
— 0

J F M A M J J A S O N D

➡ **Winter (Dec–Feb)**
Plenty of blue skies but can be extremely chilly at night. Riad rates go up between 20 December and 6 January.

➡ **Spring (Mar–May)**
Great time for medina escapades with temperatures hovering around 30°C. Try to avoid Easter holidays when prices jump.

➡ **Summer (Jun–Aug)**
Scorching heat and the Festival of Popular Arts comes to town.

➡ **Autumn (Sep–Nov)**
Ideal for non-sweaty souq exploring and sightseeing. Remember your umbrella in November, Marrakesh's wettest month.

Book Your Stay

➡ Marrakesh is famous for its riad accommodation. These medina guesthouses have limited space so it's advisable to book in advance.

➡ Groups of friends or families travelling together can often book an entire riad to themselves.

➡ Book a month ahead if you want to visit Marrakesh during any major European holiday.

➡ There is no shortage of budget-friendly inns and guesthouses. Cheap hotels are concentrated between Rue Bab Agnaou and Rue Riad Zitoun el-Kedim.

➡ Brand-name luxury resorts sit on the outskirts of town. The *palmeraie* (palm grove) is home to more intimate luxury villa guesthouses.

➡ Many riads and luxury hotels lower their prices mid-June to August, mid-January to mid-March and mid-November to mid-December.

➡ Light sleepers should be aware that sound travels easily in riads and you're never too far from a mosque minaret in the medina. Bring earplugs to mute slamming doors and the early morning call to prayer, or choose a hotel in the ville nouvelle.

Useful Websites

➡ **Hip Marrakech** (www.hipmarrakech.com) Riad accommodation specialist with a good range of options.

➡ **Marrakech Riads** (www.marrakech-riads.com) A selection of nine medina riads.

➡ **Marrakech Medina** (www.marrakech-medina.com) Local riad booking agency.

➡ **Lonely Planet** (www.lonelyplanet.com/morocco/marrakesh/hotels) Recommendations and bookings.

Best Budget

Le Gallia (www.hotellegallia.com) Great value with good-sized rooms around a citrus-tree-shaded courtyard.

Equity Point Hostel (www.equity-point.com) Swags of riad style at backpacker dorm-bed prices. Plus there's a pool.

Riad Elkarti (www.facebook.com/riadelkarti/) Arty budget riad with laid-back style.

Jnane Mogador (www.jnanemogador.com) Traditionally decorated rooms, great facilities and friendly service from owner Mohammed.

Hotel du Trésor (www.hotel-du-tresor.com) Good value riad brimming with whimsical style.

Best Midrange

Riad Le J (www.riadlej.com) Colourful, quirky design offsets Moroccan artistry at this uber-hip retreat behind the Mouassine fountain.

Riad Bledna (www.riadbledna.com) Peaceful countryside hideaway within easy reach of the city.

Tchaikana (www.tchaikana.com) Nomadic artefacts combine with swish design to create a medina pad with globe-trotting spirit.

Dar Zaman (www.darzaman.com) Snug, stylish rooms and extraordinary service.

Riad UP (www.riadup.com) Mallorcan chic meets medina living at Elsa Bauza's colourful, minimalist haven.

Dar Attajmil (www.darattajmil.com) Relaxed riad with attentive staff and small but sleek rooms.

Best Top End

Riad Azoulay (www.riad-azoulay.com) Charming service and sumptuous interiors await.

Riad L'Orangeraie (www.riadorangeraie.com) A classy home-from-home with five-star service.

Riad Al Massarah (www.riadmassarah.com) Chic, stylish and with serious environmental credentials. The ultimate feel-good getaway.

Jnane Tamsa (www.jnanetamsa.com) Sustainable style never looked so good as at this *palmeraie* resort.

Casa Taos Eclectic decor and lashings of hospitality are ladled out at this villa, located just outside of town.

Arriving in Marrakesh

Marrakech Menara Airport

Small, modern **Marrakech Menara Airport** (RAK; ☎0524 44 79 10; www.marrakech.airport-authority.com; ⏱information desk 8am-6pm; 🛜) is located 6km southwest of town. Due to the growing number of international and charter flights serving Marrakesh, the airport is expanding and a second terminal is currently being built.

In the arrivals hall you'll find currency exchange, ATMs, an information desk and phone providers where you can equip yourself with a Moroccan SIM card. The currency exchange office stays open until the last flight for the night has arrived.

➡ **Airport bus 19** (Map p28; one way/return Dh30/50; ⏱6.15am-9.30pm) runs a circular route, every 30 minutes, between the airport and central Marrakesh. From the airport, it stops at Pl de Foucauld (a one-minute walk to Djemaa el-Fna), then runs along Ave Mohammed V via Bab Nkob (alight for Bab Doukkala) to Guéliz (passing Pl du 16 Novembre and the train station) before heading back to the airport.

➡ A petit taxi to central Marrakesh from the airport (6km) should be no more than Dh70, but you will most likely have extreme difficulty convincing the driver of this. Late at night, with no other options available, drivers will typically quote between Dh120 and Dh150.

➡ If it's your first time in Marrakesh, and particularly if you're staying in a medina riad or out in the *palmeraie*, it makes sense to pay extra and organise a private airport transfer to your accommodation. Most riads charge around Dh150 to Dh170 for the service which, if you're heading into the medina, includes being met at the taxi drop-off point (usually Djemaa el-Fna) and being walked to the door.

Marrakesh Train Station

Marrakesh's **train station** (☎0524 44 77 68; www.oncf.ma; cnr Ave Hassan II & Blvd Mohammed VI) is big, organised and convenient, with ATMs, cafes and fast-food outlets.

➡ Taxis wait just outside. To Djemaa el-Fna it's no more than Dh20 on the meter (Dh30 at night) but drivers are notorious for not putting the meter on. Dh50 is the usual quoted price.

➡ Walk away from the station and hail a taxi on the street to get a better rate.

➡ Most hotels can arrange a driver to pick you up from the station.

➡ City buses 8 and 10 (Dh4) head down Av Hassan II and Av Mohammed V to Djemaa el-Fna roughly every 20 minutes between 6am and 10pm.

CTM Bus Station

The **CTM bus station** (Map p106; ☎0524 43 44 02; www.ctm.ma; Rue Abou Bakr Seddiq; ⏱6am-10pm) is located southwest of the train station (about 15 minutes on foot). There's not much at the station in the way of facilities, beyond a smoky 24-hour cafe with stuttering wi-fi. Some CTM buses also stop at the **Gare Routière** (Bus Station; ☎0524 43 39 33; Bab Doukkala), just outside the medina walls.

➡ A taxi from the station to Djemaa el-Fna

shouldn't cost more than Dh30 (drivers will often quote Dh50).

→ For a better taxi rate, walk up to Ave Hassan II and hail on the street, or catch either city buses 8 or 10 as they trundle down the road.

→ If you've disembarked at the Gare Routière, it's a 20-minute walk to Djemaa el-Fna.

Getting Around

Bus

→ Join the locals with your sardine impersonation on the city buses. Cheap and frequent but hot and overcrowded.

→ Useful for hops between Guéliz and the medina if you have a high discomfort threshold.

→ City bus tickets cost Dh4 one way.

→ Buses 8 and 10 travel between Djemaa el-Fna and the train station; bus 1 heads to Guéliz from the kasbah; bus 12 hops between Jardin Majorelle and Bab Doukkala.

→ Services start around 6am and finish between 9.30pm and 10pm; buses on most routes run every 15 to 20 minutes.

Calèche

→ These green horse-drawn carriages congregate at Pl de Foucauld next to Djemaa el-Fna.

→ State-fixed rates of Dh120 per hour apply (rates are posted inside the carriage).

→ Expect a tour of the ramparts to take 1½ hours.

→ Avoid Marrakesh rush hours (8am, noon and 5.30pm to 7.30pm).

Car & Motorcycle

→ In the medina there are guarded car parks on Rue Fatima Zohra (near Djemaa el-Fna), Rue Riad Zitoun el-Jedid (near Bahia Palace), and Rue Abbes Sebti (behind the Koutoubia Mosque).

→ In Guéliz there's a secure underground car park on Av Mohammed V, opposite the post office.

→ Expect to pay Dh20 to Dh40 per day for parking.

→ In Guéliz some roads have parking meters (Dh2 per hour). If you find street parking without a meter, a guardian will expect a Dh10 tip for keeping an eye on your car

Taxi

→ Creamy-beige petits taxis (local taxis) are abundant and the quickest way to nip around town.

→ You can hail taxis on the street or hire from a rank.

→ Trips between the medina and central Guéliz shouldn't cost more than Dh20 during the day or Dh30 at night.

Essential Information

Business Hours

→ Marrakesh businesses follow the Monday-to-Friday working week.

→ On Fridays (the main prayer day), many businesses take an extended lunch break.

→ In the medina souqs many workshops and stalls take Friday off instead of Sunday.

→ During Ramadan the rhythm of the city changes and office hours shift to around 10am to 3pm or 4pm.

Normal opening hours:

Banks 8.30am to 6.30pm Monday to Friday

Post offices 8.30am to 4.30pm Monday to Friday

Government offices 8.30am to 6.30pm Monday to Friday

Restaurants noon to 3pm and 7pm to 10pm

Bars 6pm till late

Shops 9am to 12.30pm and 2.30pm to 8pm Monday to Saturday

Electricity

Type C
220V/50Hz

Type E
220V/50Hz

Emergency

Ambulance ✆150

Brigade Touristique (Map p28; ✆0524 38 46 01; Rue Ouadi el-Makhazine)

Police ✆190

Polyclinique du Sud (Map p106; ✆0524 44 79 99; 2 Rue de Yougoslavie; ⊙24hr) Private hospital.

Money

➜ Moroccan dirham (Dh) notes come in denominations of Dh20, Dh50, Dh100 and Dh200.

➜ Dirham coins come in denominations of Dh1, Dh2, Dh5 and Dh10.

➜ The dirham is divided into 100 centimes. You may infrequently see coins in denominations of 10, 20 and 50 centimes.

➜ The dirham is a restricted currency, meaning that it cannot be taken out of the country and is not available abroad.

➜ Hang on to exchange/ATM receipts. You'll need them to convert leftover dirham at banks or exchange bureaus before you leave.

ATMs

➜ Virtually all ATMs (*guichets automatiques*) accept Visa, MasterCard, Electron, Cirrus, Maestro and InterBank cards.

➜ Most ATMs will dispense no more than Dh2000 at a time.

➜ On Sundays, ATMs on Rue Bab Agnaou (near Djemaa el-Fna) and in Rahba Kedima often run out of funds. Try ATMs on Rue Fatima Zohra near Bab Ksour, or in the ville nouvelle.

Cash

➜ The medina souqs are still very much a cash society. Only larger shops will accept credit and debit cards.

➜ Many midrange and top-end accommodations accept payment in euros.

Credit Cards

➜ Major credit cards are usually accepted at midrange and top-end accommodation, and large tourist-oriented restaurants and shops.

➜ Credit cards often incur a surcharge of around 5%.

Money Changers

➜ Most banks change cash. Travellers cheques are pretty much impossible to change.

➜ Private *bureaux de change* (exchange bureaus) offer official exchange rates and are open longer hours.

➜ Hotel Ali, near Djemaa el-Fna, nearly always offers fractionally better rates than anywhere else.

➜ Euros, US dollars and British pounds are the most easily exchanged currencies.

Public Holidays

Banks, post offices and most shops shut on the main public holidays, but transport still runs.

New Year's Day (1 January)

Independence Manifesto (11 January) Commemorates the publication in Fez of the Moroccan nationalist manifesto for independence.

Labour Day (1 May)

Feast of the Throne (30 July) Commemorates King Mohammed VI's accession to the throne.

Allegiance of Oued Eddahab (14 August) Celebrates the 'return to the fatherland' of the Oued Eddahab region in the far south.

Anniversary of the King's and People's Revolution (20 August) Commemorates the exile of Mohammed V by the French in 1953.

Young People's Day (21 August) Celebrates the king's birthday.

Anniversary of the Green March (6 November) Commemorates the Green March 'reclaiming' the Western Sahara on November 1975.

Independence Day (18 November) Commemorates independence from France.

Major Islamic Holidays

The rhythms of Islamic practice are tied to the lunar calendar so the Islamic calendar begins around 11 days earlier than the preceding year. Dates are approximate as they rely on the sighting of the new moon.

HOLIDAY	2017	2018	2019	2020
Moulid an-Nabi	1 Dec	20 Nov	9 Nov	29 Oct
Ramadan begins	27 May	16 May	6 May	24 Apr
Eid al-Fitr	25 Jun	16 Jun	4 Jun	24 May
Eid al-Adha	1 Sep	21 Aug	11 Aug	31 Jul
New Year begins (year)	21 Sep (1439)	11 Sep (1440)	31 Aug (1441)	20 Aug (1442)

Safe Travel

Marrakesh is, in general, a safe city. Hustlers and touts, though, are part and parcel of the medina experience; keep your wits about you and be prepared for a fair amount of hassle.

➡ Pickpockets work on Djemaa el-Fna and, to a lesser extent, around the medina. Carry only the minimum amount of cash necessary.

➡ Be particularly vigilant if walking around the medina at night.

➡ Hustlers and unofficial guides hang around the medina. They can be persistent and sometimes unpleasant. Maintain your good humour and be polite when declining offers of help.

Telephone

➡ To call Marrakesh from inside Morocco, always dial Marrakesh's four-digit area code (⏻0524) even when in Marrakesh.

➡ To call Marrakesh from overseas, dial your international access code + ⏻212 + ⏻524.

➡ Moroccan landlines begin with ⏻05; mobile numbers start with ⏻06.

Mobile Phones

➡ GSM phones work on roaming.

➡ If you have an unlocked mobile phone you can buy a prepaid Moroccan mobile SIM card.

Morocco's three GSM network providers are Maroc Telecom, Meditel and Inwi.

➡ SIM cards can be bought at the airport on arrival, at any of the mobile network provider stores and also from roving vendors (wearing the branded clothing of the mobile network) who hang out near the network stores and on the Rue Bab Agnaou entry to Djemaa el-Fna. Take your passport when purchasing.

➡ Prepaid packages vary; for Dh100 you can get 200 call minutes plus 10GB data. Many packages do not offer international SMS. Data coverage in Marrakesh is reliable and reasonably fast.

➡ Scratch cards to top up your credit can be bought at newsstands, grocery stores and *téléboutiques* (private phone offices).

Toilets

➡ Public toilets are scattered throughout the medina. Most are decently clean. Look for the 'WC' signs. Otherwise, head to a cafe.

Tipping

Tipping is an integral part of Moroccan life; almost any service can warrant a tip. Although you shouldn't feel railroaded, the judicious distribution of a few dirham for a service willingly rendered can make your life a lot easier.

➡ **Restaurants** 10% is standard.

➡ **Cafes** Dh2.

➡ **Museum guides** Dh10; more for great service.

➡ **Bag porters** Dh3 to Dh5 is standard.

➡ **Public-toilet attendants** Leave Dh1 to Dh2.

➡ **Car-park attendants** Dh3 to Dh5; Dh10 for overnight.

Dos & Don'ts

➔ **Do** always ask before taking a photo of locals.

➔ **Don't** drink alcohol on the street or in public spaces.

➔ **Do** cover knees and shoulders when in the medina, whether you're a man or woman; it shows your respect for your Moroccan hosts.

➔ **Don't** eat or smoke in public during daylight hours in Ramadan.

➔ **Do** learn basic greetings. A few words in Darija (Moroccan Arabic) will delight your hosts.

➔ **Don't** skip pleasantries. Always say hello before asking for help or prices.

➔ **Don't** overtly display affection to your partner in public. Hand-holding is fine; kissing is not.

➔ Public toilets and toilets in cafes and restaurants often have no toilet paper (*papier hygiénique*), so keep a supply with you.

➔ Don't throw the paper into the toilet as the plumbing is often dodgy; instead discard it in the bin provided.

Tourist Information

Office National Maro-cain du Tourisme (ONMT; Map p106; ☎ 0524 43 61 79; Pl Abdel Moumen ben Ali, Guéliz; ⊗ 8.30am–noon & 2.30-8pm Mon-Thu, 8.30-11.30am & 3-6.30pm Fri) Offers pamphlets but little in the way of actual information.

Travellers with Disabilities

Marrakesh has few facilities for the disabled, but is not necessarily out of bounds for travellers with a physical disability and a sense of adventure. Some factors to be aware of:

➔ Narrow medina streets and rutted pavements can make mobility challenging.

➔ Only a handful of top-end hotels have accessible rooms for guests with disabilities.

➔ Booking ground-floor rooms is essential as few hotels have lifts.

➔ Travellers with vision or hearing impairment are poorly catered for. Hearing loops, Braille signs and talking pedestrian crossings are nonexistent.

For further, general information on travelling with a disability, download Lonely Planet's free *Accessible Travel* guide from http://lptravel.to/AccessibleTravel.

Visas

➔ Border formalities are fairly quick and straight-forward.

➔ Most visitors do not require a visa to visit Morocco and are allowed to remain in the country for 90 days.

➔ Your passport must be valid for at least six months beyond your date of entry.

Language

The official language in Morocco is Arabic, which is used throughout the country. Berber is spoken in the Rif and Atlas Mountains. Most Berbers also speak at least some Arabic. French is still regularly used in the cities.

To enhance your trip with a phrasebook, visit **lonelyplanet.com**. Lonely Planet iPhone phrasebooks are available through the Apple App store.

Morrocan Arabic

Moroccan Arabic (Darija) is a variety of Modern Standard Arabic (MSA), but is so different from it in many respects as to be virtually like another language. This is the everyday spoken language you'll hear when in Morocco. Here, we've represented the Arabic phrases with the Roman alphabet using a simplified pronunciation system.

Basics

Hello.	es salaam alaykum (polite)
	wa alaykum salaam (reponse)
Goodbye.	bessalama/m'a ssalama
Please.	'afak/'afik/'afakum (said to m/f/pl)
Thank you.	shukran
You're welcome.	la shukran 'la wejb
Excuse me.	smeh leeya
Yes./No.	eeyeh/la
How are you?	keef halek?
Fine, thank you.	bekheer, lhamdoo llaah

Eating & Drinking

A table for..., please.
tabla dyal... 'afak

Can I see the menu, please?
nazar na'raf lmaakla lli 'andkum?

What do you recommend?
shnoo tansaani nakul?

I'll try what she/he is having.
gha nzharrab shnoo kaatakul hiyya/ huwwa

I'm a vegetarian.
makanakoolsh llehem

Shopping

I'd like to buy...	bgheet nshree...
I'm only looking.	gheer kanshoof
Can I look at it?	wakhkha nshoofha?
How much is it?	bshhal?

Emergencies

Help!	'teqnee!
Go away!	seer fhalek!
I'm lost.	tweddert
Thief!	sheffar!
I've been robbed.	tsreqt
Call the police!	'ayyet 'la lbùlees!
Call a doctor!	'ayyet 'la shee tbeeb!
There's been an accident!	uq'at kseeda!
Where's the toilet?	feen kayn lbeet lma?
I'm sick.	ana mreed
I'm allergic to (penicillin).	'andee lhasaseeya m'a (lbeenseleen)

Time & Numbers

What time is it?	shal fessa'a?
yesterday	lbareh
today	lyoom
tomorrow	ghedda
morning	fessbah
afternoon	fel'sheeya
evening	'sheeya
day	nhar
week	l'usbu'
month	shshhar
year	l'am

Transport & Directions

I'd like a ... ticket.	'afak bgheet wahed lwarka l ddar lbayda...
Where is the ...?	feen kayn ...?
airport	mataar
bus station	mhetta dyal ttobeesat
bus stop	blasa dyal ttobeesat
ticket office	maktab lwerqa
train station	lagaar
What's the fare?	shhal taman lwarka?

Please tell me when we get to ...
'atak eela wselna l ... goolhaleeya

Please wait for me.
tsennanee 'afak

Stop here, please.
wqef henna 'afak

Berber

There are three main dialects among Berber speakers, which in a certain sense also serve as loose lines of ethnic demarcation. The following phrases are a selection from the Tashelhit dialect, the one visitors are likely to find most useful.

Basics

Hello.	la bes darik/darim (m/f)
Goodbye.	akayaoon arbee
Please.	barakalaufik
Thank you.	barakalaufik
Yes.	yah
No.	oho
Excuse me.	samhiy

Practicalities

food	teeremt
somewhere to sleep	kra lblast mahengane
water	arman
Do you have...?	ees daroon ...?
How much is it?	minshk aysker?
I want to go to...	addowghs...
Where is (the)...?	mani gheela...?
straight	neeshan
to the left	fozelmad
to the right	fofasee
mountain	adrar
river	aseef
yesterday	eedgam
today	(zig sbah) rass
tomorrow	(ghasad) aska

Behind the Scenes

Send Us Your Feedback

We love to hear from travellers – your comments help make our books better. We read every word, and we guarantee that your feedback goes straight to the authors. Visit **lonelyplanet.com/contact** to submit your updates and suggestions.

Note: We may edit, reproduce and incorporate your comments in Lonely Planet products such as guidebooks, websites and digital products, so let us know if you don't want your comments reproduced or your name acknowledged. For a copy of our privacy policy visit lonelyplanet.com/privacy.

Jessica's Thanks

A huge *shukran* to all the Marrakshis who always make coming to Marrakesh such a pleasure. Big thanks to Youssef, Fatima, Hasan and Amine; to Mark for a lowdown on the local scene over beers; Cyril for tips and advice; and in particular to Mohammed Nour for taking time out of his schedule to help out. Also thanks to Virginia and Peter for restaurant-checking fun.

Acknowledgements

Cover photograph: Cycling through the medina, Marrakesh, Hemis/AWL ©

Contents photograph: Djemaa el-Fna, Marrakesh, Matthew Williams-Ellis/ Creative ©

This Book

This 4th edition of Lonely Planet's *Pocket Marrakesh* guidebook was researched and written by Jessica Lee. The previous edition was also researched and written by Jessica Lee. This guidebook was produced by the following:

Destination Editor Helen Elfer

Product Editors Susan Paterson, Martine Power

Senior Cartographer David Kemp

Book Designer Jessica Rose

Assisting Editors Imogen Bannister, Janice Bird, Christopher Pitts, Tracy Whitmey

Cover Researcher Naomi Parker

Thanks to Chas Bayfield, Zoe Etim, Liz Heynes, Claire Naylor, Karyn Noble, Lauren O'Connell, Kirsten Rawlings, Ellie Simpson, Tony Wheeler

Index

See also separate subindexes for:

⊗ **Eating p157**

☻ **Drinking p158**

☺ **Entertainment p158**

🔒 **Shopping p158**

Sights **000**
Map Pages **000**

Our Writer

Jessica Lee

Jess high-tailed it for the road at the age of 18 and hasn't looked back since. In 2011 she swapped a career as an adventure-tour leader for travel writing and since then her travels for Lonely Planet have taken her across Africa, the Middle East and Asia. She tweets @jessofarabia. Jess has contributed to Lonely Planet's *Egypt, Turkey, Cyprus, Morocco, Middle East, Europe, Africa, Cambodia* and *Vietnam* guidebooks and her travel writing has appeared in *Wanderlust* magazine, the *Daily Telegraph,* the *Independent, BBC Travel* and on lonelyplanet.com.

Published by Lonely Planet Global Limited
CRN 554153
4th edition – Aug 2017
ISBN 978 1 78657 036 9
© Lonely Planet 2017 Photographs © as indicated 2017
10 9 8 7 6 5 4 3 2
Printed in Malaysia